ROMAN
DORSET

ROMAN
DORSET

BILL PUTNAM

The History Press

For Maureen

First published 2007
Reprinted 2011

The History Press
The Mill, Brimscombe Port
Stroud, Gloucestershire, GL5 2QG
www.thehistorypress.co.uk

British Library Cataloguing in Publication Data.
A catalogue record for this book is available from the British Library.

ISBN 978 0 7524 4104 7

Typesetting and origination by The History Press
Printed in Great Britain

CONTENTS

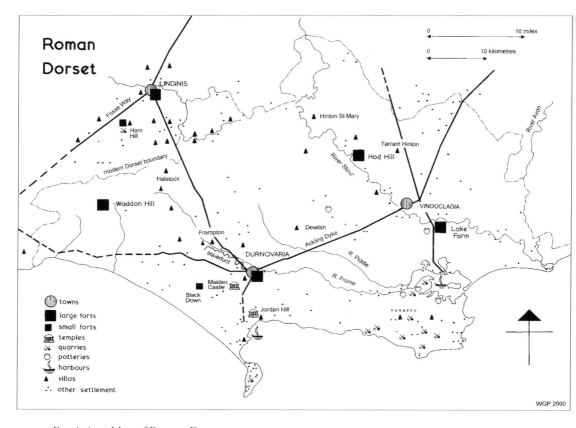

Frontispiece: Map of Roman Dorset

PREFACE AND ACKNOWLEDGEMENTS

This book is the result of 40 years of fieldwork and practical research by the author in Dorset, and hopefully it will be of use both to inhabitants of Dorset and to visitors to the county. Although it is written in a popular style, those engaged in research into Roman Britain in general will be able to find material that is otherwise not yet easily available in print, such as the Roman town house in Dorchester and the author's own work on the Dorchester Roman Aqueduct and the Dewlish Roman Villa.

The author is grateful for the help of many friends and past students in preparing this book, especially Maureen Putnam, checker of details and adviser-in-chief.

Grateful thanks are also due to the following: Francesca Radcliffe for the aerial photographs of the aqueduct, Maumbury Rings and Grimstone Down, Peter Leach for the map of Ilchester, the Dorset Natural History and Archaeological Society, Dorset County Museum and Katherine Barker, editor of the *Proceedings of the Dorset Natural History & Archaeological Society* for permission to use much material from their publications and archives, Steve Cosh for his expert assessment of the Dewlish mosaic pavements, Martin Papworth and the National Trust for material on *Vindocladia*, John Hodgson for his brilliant reconstruction drawings which bring Roman Dorset to life, Ted Flatters for his photo of Dorset County Museum, and Wessex Archaeology for photographs of artefacts from their excavations in Dorchester. If any copyright material has inadvertently been used without permission, the author apologises and will be pleased to correct this in any future edition.

LIST OF ILLUSTRATIONS

COLOUR PLATES

MONOCHROME FIGURES

1

THE DUROTRIGES

At first sight it may seem incongruous to talk of 'Roman Dorset', when Dorset is a modern county division of England. However, a group of people with a distinct identity can be traced in Dorset, certainly as far back as the Iron Age, and probably even earlier. Human settlement has existed in Dorset since at least 4000 BC. The inhabitants of the Neolithic (New Stone Age) and Bronze Ages built the burial mounds which are still a prominent feature of the landscape. Recent research has made it clear that the site of Dorchester and its immediate surroundings has been an important centre of human activity since the Neolithic period.

At Mount Pleasant on the south-eastern edge of Dorchester lies one of the great 'henge' monuments of the period around 2000 BC, when a series of such religious and political structures was created across many parts of England. The most famous is of course Stonehenge, after which the sites have been named, but Avebury is a closer parallel to Mount Pleasant. The major difference is that the upright structures at Mount Pleasant were of timber while those at Avebury were of sarsen stone. Within the circle formed by the bank and ditch at Mount Pleasant was a circular pattern of postholes which almost certainly represented a large circular building, similar to that at Woodhenge which was found near yet another great henge at Durrington Walls in Wiltshire.

But this was not all. Another henge of a different character was built at Maumbury Rings on the outskirts of modern Dorchester. Little of this is visible today, as the Roman army converted the conveniently sized enclosing bank into an amphitheatre, which masks its prehistoric origins. Here there were no upright stones or posts, rather deep pits which perhaps attempted to make contact with the gods of the underworld.

During the construction of the Waitrose supermarket in Dorchester itself further evidence was found of the importance of this area during the Late Neolithic and Early Bronze Age. A series of huge posts stood at intervals of 5m in postholes 3m deep. It is possible that these formed part of another very large timber circle, but it is perhaps more likely that they were one side of an avenue leading from the River Frome to Mount Pleasant or Maumbury Rings. Such an arrangement is paralleled at Stonehenge and particularly at Avebury.

By the Iron Age, which started early in the first millennium BC, it is clear that 'Dorset' had arrived. It becomes possible through the distribution of pottery and eventually of

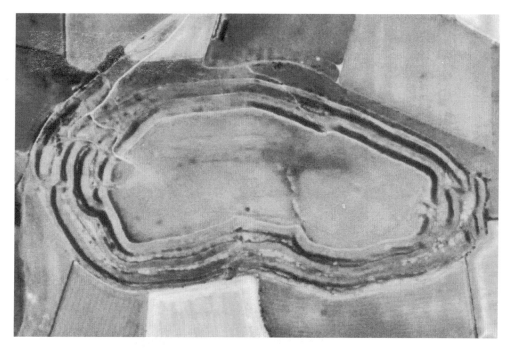

1 Aerial photograph of the hillfort of Maiden Castle

coins to define the territory of the people of Dorset, and with the help of the Romans to give them a name. They were the Durotriges. Their territory was a little larger than modern Dorset. It extended to the Avon in the east, the Wylye in the north and at least as far as the Axe in the west. The hillforts of Ham Hill and South Cadbury, both in Somerset, were certainly Durotrigian. The Durotriges were the major hillfort builders of Britain. Hillforts exist almost everywhere, but nowhere in such numbers and size as in their territory. The sites include Maiden Castle (*1*), Hod Hill, Hambledon, Eggardon, Badbury Rings and many others. No one has attempted to calculate the amount of earth shifted, but it was enormous. The Roman historian Suetonius, describing the attack on south-west Britain by the future emperor Vespasian, says he captured 20 towns (*oppida*). By this Suetonius surely means the hillforts of the Durotriges.

The question of what was inside the hillforts depends partly on excavations, and partly on surface evidence from those which have not been ploughed. A small hillfort which is unploughed is Abbotsbury Castle. Here you can still see the ring of 11 circular huts which housed the inhabitants. There is a vast amount of empty space. One idea is that in times of trouble other farmers from the surrounding countryside would take refuge in the hillfort, bringing their livestock with them.

Among the large hillforts, Hod Hill, north of Blandford, offers important evidence. Most of this site has now been ploughed at one time or another, but a famous aerial photograph taken in 1924 before most of the ploughing, shows that this major hillfort was closely covered with round huts, with streets showing clearly between them.

Excavation at Maiden Castle suggests a similar intensive occupation. In fact these hillforts were in the process of developing into towns. Among the more advanced tribes of south-east England such towns were already in existence, such as that at Prae Wood in Hertfordshire, which wasn't even situated on a hilltop. At Danebury near Stockbridge in Hampshire, excavation has shown that by the time of the Roman conquest, the hillfort had been abandoned for more comfortable places to live. This hillfort belonged to the Atrebates.

It is not yet clear whether this was true of Dorset. The hillforts were clearly defended against the Romans. But were they still the great centres of political activity that they had been? There were extensive and crowded settlements on the land between Maiden Castle and Dorchester, but it is not yet clear whether these settlements appeared before or after the Roman conquest. It has recently been suggested that a major settlement already existed on the site of Dorchester itself before the construction of the Roman town *Durnovaria*. This is a very interesting hypothesis, but at present there is little evidence to support it.

It may seem surprising that we can put a name to a prehistoric tribe at all. But though their early days were before history, once the people came into contact with the Greek and Roman world – and this happened through trade long before the invasion of AD 43 – then written records of their name became possible. Even so, we are lucky to know their name, and it occurs in only three places; on two building inscriptions put up by Durotrigian work parties on Hadrian's Wall, and in the *Geography* of Ptolemy, a Greek writing in Alexandria about AD 150. Ptolemy and one of the wall stones calls them Durotriges (*2, 3*); another wall stone (from Housesteads) calls them Durotrages. Durotrages must remain a possibility, but they are usually known as the Durotriges.

Since we know so little of them, how can we define their territory? There are two main ways of doing this: first by the location of finds of their characteristic dark brown or Black Burnished pottery, and secondly by finds of their own distinctive coins (*4, 5*). These were silver staters and quarter-staters, but unlike the tribes in south-eastern Britain, they had not taken to inscribing their kings' names or names of their cities in Latin letters. As far as we know, they were illiterate.

In the last centuries before the Roman conquest they were certainly engaged in trade with the continent, particularly the Armorican peninsula (Brittany). Coins of Armorican tribes are occasionally found in Dorset, and large quantities of continental pottery were imported through the trading centre in the promontory fort at Hengistbury Head (Cunliffe 1987). The Durotriges almost certainly helped Armorica in their revolt against the Romans in 56 BC. This brought an end to the trade at Hengistbury but also provides a clue to their origins.

It used to be fashionable to imagine that every new group of people identified in Britain came here by way of violent invasion; but it is now realised that this is not necessarily the case. In origin the Durotriges were probably a mixture of the indigenous people of Dorset (themselves already a mixture) with new groups, arriving from Armorica. They came initially to trade, later to settle and intermarry with the locals. A similar process has gone on ever since.

2 Stone mentioning the Durotriges at Chesters on Hadrian's Wall

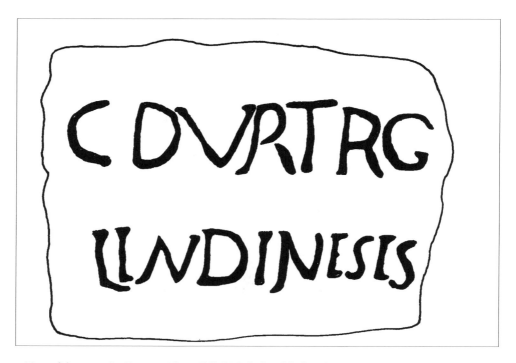

3 Text of the stone in *Figure 2*: C[IVITAS] DVR[O]TR[I]G[VM] LINDINESIS 'The civitas of the Durotriges from Ilchester'

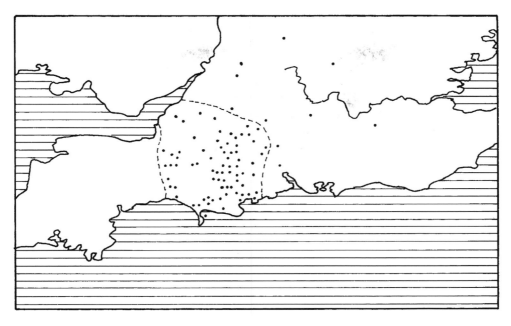

4 Distribution map of Durotrigian coins; each dot represents the spot where one or more coins have been found. The dotted line is a possible Durotrigian boundary

5 Silver coins of the Durotriges

The knowledge of iron had arrived in Dorset as early as 700 BC and this too may reflect the arrival of a group of people who became part of the Durotriges who awaited the Roman invasion in AD 43.

The Iron Age chieftains lived a life surrounded by luxurious artefacts and what can only be described as works of art, many imported from the continent. There were two artistic styles, known to us as Hallstatt and La Tène, after sites in Austria and Switzerland respectively, where such objects were first recognised. La Tène follows Hallstatt somewhere about 500 BC. The La Tène style is the most spectacular. The patterns are abstract geometric designs involving swooping reverse curves and circles. The most spectacular piece found in Dorset is the bronze mirror (6) from Portesham near Abbotsbury, which can now be seen in Dorset County Museum. Although buried shortly after the Roman conquest, it represented the height of fashion in the Late Iron Age. On its back was a beautiful pattern of La Tène curves and circles. The other side was, of course, polished to act as a mirror. It was a high-status object. In the grave with the mirror and the bones of a mature lady were pots, brooches, a Roman toilet set and a Roman strainer.

In terms of quality this grave parallels the male burial at Whitcombe, south-east of Dorchester, known as the 'warrior burial', also on display in the Museum (7). He had his sword with its baldrick, a spear, a hammer and file and a spindle whorl.

One of the most successful industries of the Durotriges was the manufacture of pottery. Ball clay is still dug today in Purbeck for pottery and other industries, and in Iron Age Dorset an even larger industry flourished. 'Durotrigian' pottery is found throughout Durotrigian territory and sometimes beyond. Distinctive bowls, cups and jars were made in reducing fires (kilns were not used) and the resulting dark grey or black ware finished by burnishing. Along with their coins this is one of the ways of distinguishing Durotrigian territory. So successful was the industry that it survived the Roman conquest and obtained lucrative contracts with the Roman army, which it continued to supply with a more Romanised product, even as far afield as Hadrian's Wall.

The Iron Age, at least in Dorset, was not generally a period of spectacular burials. Beyond the lady at Portesham and the warrior at Whitcombe, both of whom were undoubtedly members of the Durotrigian 'nobility', we have only the cemeteries such as that at Maiden Castle, where the dead were buried curled up on their sides, sometimes with pots of food. This is the only indication we have of their belief in an afterlife.

Temples are known elsewhere in Iron Age Britain, but few in Durotrigian territory beyond a small rectangular one in South Cadbury Castle, and a possible circular predecessor to the later Roman temple in Maiden Castle. It is possible, but not certain by any means, that the magnificent Cerne Giant represents one of the gods of the Durotriges, standing as he does in a busy Iron Age landscape of fields and farms. There are parallels in other parts of Britain to show that Iron Age people found deities in natural places like rivers, lakes and forests.

One of the most famous is the bog at Llyn Cerrig Bach in Anglesey. In this had been deposited as a votive offering a large hoard of La Tène items, including swords, spears, shields, chariot fittings, slave chains, a bronze trumpet and currency bars. There is

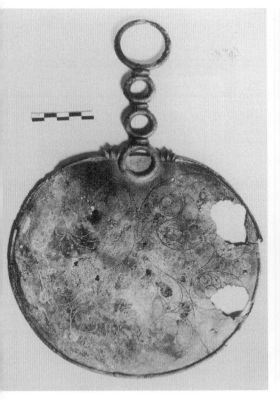

Above left: 6 Bronze Mirror of a Durotrigian lady, found at Portesham. © *Dorset County Museum*

Above right: 7 The 'Whitcombe Warrior', a Durotrigian man buried with his sword. © *Dorset County Museum*

comparatively little evidence of this sort in Dorset, but a recent excavation at Norden in Purbeck has produced a substantial hoard of Iron Age artefacts and an associated building, which may well prove to be a temple and ritual deposit of this sort.

To the Romans, the main priests among the Iron Age people were the Druids. They were regarded as unspeakable because of their practice of sacrificing humans for the good of the community. This was probably true. The Romans went to enormous lengths to wipe them and their influence out completely, but there is no evidence for their activity in Dorset.

Thus we have Durotrigian Dorset, a distinct tribal area, fiercely defended, with its own coinage entirely different from the coinage of the Belgic tribes to the east. The Durotriges had a successful pottery industry that was to rise to even greater heights under Roman control. Their kings and lesser chieftains developed and probably lived in heavily defended hillforts, which had gone some way to becoming towns. Their population was large and they were prospering. It must not be thought that they all lived in the hillforts; the whole countryside was a network of farms and villages, and the

8 Reconstruction of an Iron Age dwelling at New Barn, Bradford Peverell

small rectangular fields of their farms covered much of the landscape, including many areas which we tend to think of as being cultivated for the first time since the Second World War.

Their houses were round thatched huts of substantial size. Recent experiments in building these have shown that they could be warm and comfortable. Such huts can be seen at Butser Ancient Farm and at New Barn (*8*) near Dorchester. But all said and done, they were still an Iron Age tribe, living in what most people today would find quite intolerable conditions, close to nature and often in fear of attack. This is illustrated by one of the most common features of Iron Age sites, the grain storage pit. Here the harvest was stored; the tops were camouflaged, in the hope of saving their food in time of danger.

In the early summer of AD 43 (not that they named the years in that way!) horsemen galloped from farm to farm, warning of an impending invasion that was to take more from them than their food supplies. The value of what it brought to them is a matter of debate.

2

THE ROMAN CONQUEST

In AD 43 the Durotriges suffered one of the most frightening experiences ever to befall the county. The Romans had for many years ruled over the tribes in Gaul and to some extent in Germany. In fact the Gauls were themselves half-Roman by now, the great days of Vercingetorix's revolt against Caesar already beyond living memory. But the Channel, part of the Roman 'Ocean' which surrounded their known world, lay between the Romans and the island of *Britannia*. Caesar, after enormous difficulty with the tides in the Channel (unfamiliar to Mediterranean sailors) had raided Britain in 55 BC, and returned in 54 to conquer the south-eastern part, including its king Cassivellaunus and his possible capital at Wheathampstead.

Political and military pressures on the continent took him back to Rome and the British conquest did not survive, in contrast to Gaul which became part of the Roman Empire at that time. For 97 years the tribes of Britain remained independent, though with increasing trade connections with the Roman world. Then, in AD 43, another Roman ruler, the emperor Claudius, found it expedient to return to Britain and complete Caesar's conquest. Many have wondered why he did it. Archaeological evidence can rarely supply the answer to such a question, but there is a remarkable inscription which is kept in the Capitoline Museum in Rome, which makes clear the importance of the conquest of Britain to the emperor. It comes from the triumphal arch of Claudius, erected in AD 52. Some written history also survives, especially the *Histories* of Dio Cassius.

This evidence makes it clear that Claudius needed a military victory to gain the support of the soldiers on whom his power depended and probably this was the main reason behind the invasion. A pretext occurred in the form of an appeal for Roman help from a British prince, and the invasion began in early July.

THE INVASION

Claudius did not initially command in person, but appointed his best general, Aulus Plautius, to command the army and become the first governor of the new province. Four legions crossed the Channel. They were *II Augusta*, *IX Hispana*, *XIV Gemina* and

XX Valeria. All were drawn from other provinces where they were not needed. A legion was between 5000 and 6000 strong, and since they would have been accompanied by a similar number of auxiliary troops (archers, slingers, light infantry and cavalry) the total size of the force was about 45,000 men.

The Roman intelligence services had learnt much from Caesar's experience and trading contacts since that time. Few mistakes were made and by early September Claudius had arrived in person to take charge in response to a pre-planned 'appeal' for help from Aulus Plautius. Claudius routed the enemy, who were led by Cogodumnus and Caractacus, the sons of Cunobelinus (known as Cymbeline in Shakespeare's play). He then entered Colchester in triumph. Colchester (*Camulodunum*) had by then become the capital of the Catuvellauni, the dominant tribe of southern Britain.

The Catuvellauni had themselves presented a threat to the Durotriges, but they and the other tribes of the south-east were all defeated or had submitted to suit their own ends. We do not know the exact movements of the four legions, but late in the year a legion which was almost certainly II Augusta was sending its supplies ashore at Chichester, and setting up bases on the fringe of the already conquered territory of the Atrebates to the east.

The Durotriges not surprisingly resisted grimly. They had had little contact with the Roman government and as far as we know had not been involved in the political manoeuvrings of recent years. The Roman invaders represented a threat as fearsome as that presented to the British by the German armies in 1940.

The Romans planned, at least initially, a province formed from the more developed Belgic tribes of the south-east, but for military reasons the frontier was drawn along a line from Lincoln to Seaton in Devon, and we now know that frontier as the Fosse Way. Unfortunately for the Durotriges, their territory was within the frontier; in any case their heavily fortified hilltop towns could not be left untouched on the Romans' southern flank.

THE WAR AGAINST THE DUROTRIGES

The result was a bitter war of conquest fought over a considerable period and possibly culminating in a last rebellion at the time of Boudica's campaign of AD 60, which left its bloody remains in the gateway of the hillfort at South Cadbury in Somerset (see p.34 below).

The initial forward base of *Legio II Augusta* in Durotrigian territory seems to have been at Lake Farm, on the banks of the Stour at Wimborne. Here excavations by Poole Museums along the line of the Wimborne bypass have shown a tantalising glimpse of the defences (9) and the barrack blocks of a substantial fortress. Geophysical surveys of the meadows by the river suggest that the fortress covered 12ha (about 29 acres). This is big enough for a full legion when camping briefly on the march, but with wooden barrack blocks as were seen in the excavation, only part of the legion can have been stationed there.

9 The V-shaped ditch of the Lake Farm fort under excavation

10 Commander of the Second Augustan Legion, Vespasian (later emperor), seen here on a coin

It is unclear where the auxiliary regiments which undoubtedly accompanied the legion were stationed. In later stages of the campaigns in Britain their distinctive forts of about 2-3ha can often be found positioned to control the newly conquered territory. None are known in Dorset. They may have existed, but at this stage of the conquests the auxiliary regiments may have been brigaded with legionary detachments. There is certainly evidence for this at the forts of Hod Hill and Waddon Hill (Stoke Abbot). The Lake Farm fortress is connected by a well-authenticated Roman road (see chapter 11) directly to the sea at Hamworthy, where some military stores have been found, and more recently traces of the Roman fortlet guarding the harbour.

We can name the commander (*legatus legionis*) of the Second Augustan Legion (*Legio II Augusta*) at the time of the invasion, something rarely possible in the story of Roman Britain. He was Vespasian (*10*), later to become emperor, and a very good one at that. His life is described in eulogistic terms by the writer Suetonius, who says 'he went to Britain, where he fought thirty battles, conquered two warlike tribes, and captured more than twenty towns, besides the whole of the Isle of Wight'.

We would not know where he was posted if it were not for the reference to the Isle of Wight (*Vectis insula*). It seems likely that one of the two 'warlike tribes' he conquered was the Durotriges. It is unlikely that he completed the conquest of the Durotriges in his brief stay, and the archaeological evidence suggests it took much longer. Surely the 20 *oppida* he captured were the great hillforts of the Durotriges.

THE CAMPAIGN DEVELOPS

Several of these hillforts have revealed traces of the violent assaults that occurred. Undoubtedly the most spectacular evidence is provided by Hod Hill near Blandford. Here excavations by Professor Ian Richmand for the British Museum in the 1950s suggested that one of the cohorts of *Legio II Augusta* accompanied by a regiment of cavalry was stationed here in an unusual fort built actually inside the ramparts of the Iron Age hillfort. From the air (*11*) the contour-hugging native ramparts and the neat and efficient Roman defences provide a sharp contrast. It is visually the most dramatic site in the whole of the conquest story. No one knows for sure why the Roman commander used the native defences for two sides of his enclosure. Whatever the status of Hod Hill in Iron Age Dorset, the Roman commander felt it necessary to have significant forces on the spot to prevent reoccupation and a revival of resistance. Perhaps Hod Hill was the political and religious centre of the eastern group of Durotrigian communities.

11 The Iron Age hillfort of Hod Hill, showing the Roman fort inserted in its north-west corner

Clearly the Durotrigian inhabitants were no longer there when the Roman fort was built. They were dead or scattered in the countryside waging guerrilla warfare. The excavations found many iron heads of *ballista* bolts, the mechanically fired arrows of the legion's light artillery. Significantly a large group were driven into the ground in the area of one particular native hut which had its own enclosure within the hillfort. Richmond suggested that the barrage was concentrated on the chieftain's hut. This may be so, but it cannot be confirmed as this was the only Iron Age hut excavated. The excavation concentrated on the Roman defences, which are known in considerable detail.

The Roman occupation of Hod Hill did not last long. The significant factor in assessing the importance and length of occupation is the layout of the Roman roads. When the permanent pattern of the occupation was settled and the military roads built, no road was built to Hod Hill. It had already fulfilled its purpose and the units involved moved further west. Its function was to control the newly conquered native population, and to provide a protective screen to the major site at Lake Farm and its harbour at Hamworthy. Some of the buildings at Hod Hill were burnt down, and much equipment left lying about the fort. Perhaps it ended in disaster from a Durotrigian attack, but it is all too easy to assume that burnt buildings mean an enemy attack. They may have been burnt by accident or burnt to clear the site.

A similar fort existed at Waddon Hill, Stoke Abbot, and appears to have been occupied in the early fifties till about AD 60, the year of the great Boudican rebellion. Excavations here were carried out by Dr Graham Webster in the 1960s and found a similar type of fort to Hod Hill, though this time on a site not used by the Durotriges. The fort at Waddon Hill provides an example of the use of signalling by the Roman army in its campaigns in Britain, and similar arrangements may have existed for Hod Hill. On Black Down near Hardy's Monument west of Dorchester lies a Roman fortlet, which can only be explained as an element in a signalling chain to allow the unit at Waddon Hill to raise the alarm with the fort at Dorchester (see p.28).

Excavations by the author found evidence for a small fortification of typical Roman construction on Black Down (*colour plate 4*). The rampart and V-shaped ditch were built in the same style and to the same dimensions as the rampart at Hod Hill, except that only one ditch was constructed. In the north-east corner of the fortlet there was a ramp leading up to the rampart top, presumably an *ascensus* for easy access to the rampart. There was a single entrance facing east, with two postholes for the pair of gates. The posts themselves had been levered out and the posts removed, probably for reuse. No structures were found in the interior, but there was evidence that portable prefabricated wooden buildings stood on the gravel subsoil. Pottery from contexts sealed by the rampart contained nothing later than the first century AD.

The identification of this site as a signal station depends mainly on its location (*12*). It is just far enough up the northern slope of Black Down to gain a line of sight to Dorchester in one direction and the fort at Waddon Hill in the other. This was confirmed during the excavation by the lighting of flares on the three sites involved. Furthermore it is difficult to suggest an alternative function for such a fortlet in an otherwise very odd location.

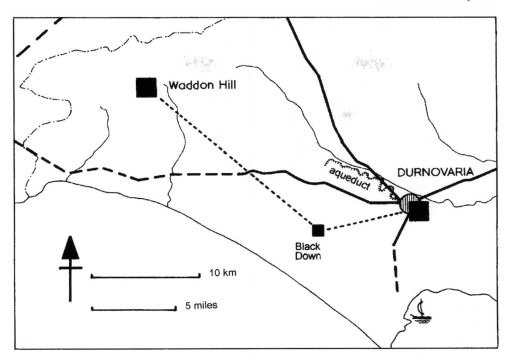

12 Map showing the chain for signalling from Waddon to Dorchester via the fortlet at Black Down

It will be seen from the map that the distance from Dorchester to Black Down is only half of that from Black Down to Waddon. It may well be that another site exists somewhere in the area of the Eggardon hillfort, but at the time of writing this has not been found. Such a signal station will only have been able to give the alarm – fire at night and smoke by day. One might argue that this would not be of much value, as an attack on Waddon would be sure to take place on a foggy day when signalling was impossible. It may be so, but there is no doubt that the Roman army used its signalling skills in Britain. The best parallel to the Black Down signal station is Robin Hood's Butt, part of the signalling chain to the outpost fort at Bewcastle on Hadrian's Wall.

Both Hod Hill and Waddon Hill are unusual: Roman forts in Britain are normally to be found on lower ground, within easy reach of road and river transport particularly at road junctions and river crossings. Hod Hill and Waddon Hill lie on hilltops, difficult of access and unconnected to the known Roman road system. This must reflect the tactical problems of the Durotrigian campaign; at times the situation may well have been one of considerable difficulty.

Other forts must have existed. Probably one has been quarried away at Ham Hill, near Ilminster. Roman military buildings existed at South Cadbury and Maiden Castle, but it is not clear how extensive they were. Yet others may exist undetected or destroyed.

THE ROMAN FORT AT DORCHESTER

Although the presence of a Roman fort at Dorchester has long been suspected, no direct trace of it has ever been found. The following is a brief outline of the evidence for its existence and an attempt to define its location. The author would be pleased to hear from others with ideas about the problem.

The reasons for suggesting that there was a fort at Dorchester are as follows:

1. The Roman roads of Dorset were built by the army for their own purposes (see chapter 11). Dorchester is at a major road junction near the crossing of the River Frome. The original road runs through the site of the later town towards the harbour at Weymouth. Two roads branch from this original road: a link road to the fort at Ilchester on the Fosse Way, and the later extension of the trunk road towards Seaton and Exeter. A fort must have been built to protect this important junction.

2. It is likely that the great hillfort of Maiden Castle had been of prime importance in Iron Age Dorset, and a fort to control the centre of Durotrigian authority would have been essential. Although there is evidence of Roman military buildings in Maiden Castle, these can not have been permanent. The road from Weymouth harbour went to Dorchester, not Maiden Castle.

3. A major indication that a Roman fort lay somewhere in the Dorchester area is to be found in the Roman amphitheatre, Maumbury Rings (see below). Excavation in the amphitheatre has shown that it was built probably in the AD 50s, long before the civilian town existed, and must therefore belong to a military site (all permanent or semi-permanent Roman forts had amphitheatres). Later, when the army had left Dorset, it became the town's amphitheatre.

4. Similarly the Dorchester Roman aqueduct (see chapter 4) has recently been shown to be military in origin, and thus originally built to supply a Roman fort and its bath house.

5. There have been military finds in and around Dorchester. A Roman sword handle made of bone (13) was found on the site of the present post office, and a soldier's belt buckle was found on the Fairfield. Coins of Claudian date have been found in various parts of Dorchester.

6. There are two other artefacts which may be connected with a Roman fort, though their significance is uncertain. At Whitcombe, near Dorchester, a carved stone was found which may be part of a cavalryman's tombstone (14). In the structure of the church at the village of Godmanstone is a reused altar stone dedicated to Jupiter Optimus Maximus by a centurion (though it appears to refer to a legion other than *II Augusta*).

13 Bone handle of a Roman sword found in Dorchester

14 Part of a sculptured relief found at Whitcombe near Dorchester, which may part of a Roman cavalryman's tombstone

15 Excavation across Bowling Alley Walk in Dorchester, on the line of the Roman town walls

There are some clues as to the location of the elusive fort, but any hypothesis has also to explain why archaeological research in Dorchester over a century and a half has failed to pinpoint the site. The Dorchester Excavation Committee and successor bodies have excavated extensively in Dorchester. Nothing has been found within the bounds of the Roman town (*Durnovaria*, tribal capital of the Durotriges) to indicate that a fort lies under the later town. A specific dig in Bowling Alley Walk (*15*) to find the ramparts of an early fort under the later town ramparts found no trace of early military activity.

This is of course surprising, as many Roman towns in Britain were founded on the site of disused military forts, but the evidence strongly suggests that the site of the Dorchester fort lay outside the later civilian town. The find sites of the Claudian coins are not well recorded, but the military buckle came from the Fairfield on the south side of the town between the south gate and the amphitheatre, and the sword handle was found at the site of the present post office, again suggesting a location on the south of the town.

Most important is the evidence of the military roads. The roads from the east, the south and the north-west all show signs of having been realigned after their initial construction. They appear originally to have pointed towards somewhere south or south-west of the town and this now appears to be the likeliest location for the fort. Most significantly the road from the east has been seen in excavations in Charles Street in Dorchester, and is clearly heading on towards the south-west of the town (see *78*).

Later the roads were realigned to the street grid of the new town. The road to Exeter is confusing and not fully understood. It also appears to have been realigned at Damers Road, but it is not clear what route it took before this. The known course of the aqueduct involves it leaving the contoured route it has followed down the Frome valley to run into the later town. If its original route is continued approximately along the 75m contour, it also runs towards the south-west of the town.

Thus a site for the fort must satisfy the following criteria:

1. The original military roads must run to its gates or pass close to them.
2. It must give easy and close access to the military amphitheatre.
3. It must lie somewhere near the original route of the military aqueduct, or at least its bath house must (the baths might easily be lower than the fort and may well be outside its ramparts).
4. It must be somewhere that could easily have been overlooked in previous research.

There seem to be two possible locations:

The Fairfield or market place was established in the 1870s, and a substantial sum was spent by the town council on levelling it for this purpose. Prior to this the area was part of the Fordington open fields, and regularly ploughed. It may well be that these activities destroyed much of the traces of the fort, though deeper ditches and foundation trenches should still be there. The site is at present laid out as a car park and much of it is covered with tarmac. Nevertheless there are accessible areas within and just outside the Fairfield, and around the amphitheatre.

Victoria Park is a pre–Second World War housing estate which lies on the high ground, mostly within the 80m contour. It is the highest ground close to the amphitheatre, and would give a fort an excellent view, including a view southwards towards Maiden Castle. It would also be possible for the military roads to run to Victoria Park. The area is all built up. Could the traces of a Roman earth and timber fort have been missed during the building work, not to mention military finds? It's certainly possible, given pressures of development. At present the only ground available for investigation would be the gardens of the larger properties.

The amphitheatre (*colour plate 1*) is perhaps the most intriguing feature in any discussion of the fort at Dorchester. The evidence for the date of its construction depends mainly on the samian pottery found in the 1908 excavations. It seems inescapable that the amphitheatre was built well before the foundation of the civilian town of *Durnovaria*. This means that it is originally a military amphitheatre or *ludus*, used for training, parades and assemblies by the Roman army.

It is comparable in size to the amphitheatre at the legionary fortress of Caerleon in South Wales. It could certainly seat 5000 men. The implication of this is that *Legio II Augusta* at one time had its headquarters at Dorchester, and the major part of the legion was present. But until fieldwork manages to define the boundaries and nature of the Roman fort at Dorchester this must remain a puzzle.

It may be relevant to ask why the later town was not founded on the abandoned fort site, as in so many other cases in Roman Britain. The answer may be that as the fort was legionary headquarters and was responsible for the administration of the Durotriges, the site was not yet available when the construction of the town began. The fort's *vicus*, or extramural civil settlement, may have provided the starting point.

One of the exciting things about archaeology is that at any moment a new discovery may throw into confusion one's most cherished ideas, and perhaps by the time these words appear in print some new discovery will have been made, which clears up the mystery of the Roman fort at Dorchester, or perhaps puts the problem in a new light.

MAIDEN CASTLE

It would more likely have been from a temporary camp that the Romans launched their attack on Maiden Castle, certainly the most famous of the Durotrigian hillforts. Sir Mortimer Wheeler's excavations (Wheeler 1944) here in the late 1930s suggested some grim details about the Roman assault. He depicted the Durotrigians attempting in vain to defend their hillfort against an army which was trained and equipped to storm much more sophisticated defences than those of Maiden Castle.

However, re-excavation of some of Wheeler's trenches by Niall Sharples in 1985-6 (Sharples 1991) and recent research on the skeletons from the cemetery make it clear that there is little real evidence for a Roman assault, far less in fact than at Hod Hill. A small number of *ballista* bolts were found, but not in the firing pattern found at Hod Hill. The crucial factor is the cemetery. It was the first time that a Durotrigian cemetery had been

16 A Roman *ballista* bolt still in the spine of a native defender of Maiden Castle. © *Dorset County Museum*

excavated and signs of injury and apparently hasty burial suggested the aftermath of a great battle. But it is now clear that this style of interment was normal among the Durotriges, and this was one of the major cemeteries of the hillfort, used over a considerable period. With a few exceptions the injuries visible on some skeletons are not the result of battle against the Romans, but more likely the result of accident or an apparent culture which involved duelling. Some were buried with food for their journey to another world.

The main exceptions were several skeletons which had been killed either by the *pilum* of a Roman legionary or by a Roman *ballista* bolt. One skeleton with the head of a *ballista* bolt still in his spine is dramatically displayed in the exhibit in Dorset County Museum (*16*). However, although these Durotrigian fighters may well have been killed on the ramparts of Maiden Castle, they could easily have been killed elsewhere and brought home for burial. We know all too little about the detailed circumstances of the conquest. Perhaps we should imagine the king or queen of the Durotriges, after hearing of the fate of Hod Hill, meeting the Roman commander and signing a surrender. It is quite impossible to know for certain.

THE END OF THE MILITARY PHASE

It is a mistake to imagine the Roman army patrolling Dorset throughout the three and a half centuries that Britain was part of the Roman Empire. There is at present no evidence of any of the forts being occupied after about AD 65, and even the legionary fortress at Exeter is abandoned soon after that, and the Second Augustan Legion (*Legio II Augusta*) moved finally (in AD 75) to its permanent home in Caerleon in South Wales.

By the mid-seventies the civilian towns were being built and Romanisation was in full swing. Clearly by then the battle was won by the Romans, and Dorset was becoming fully integrated into the Roman world. The soldiers moved away to the north, where they remained permanently on guard.

But at least in the north of the territory of the Durotriges there is evidence at South Cadbury which suggests a last stand, which left its dead lying unburied in the south-west gateway. This may have been in AD 60, when Boudica, Queen of the Iceni of Norfolk, led her people and many others in a final attempt to gain their freedom. All available Roman troops were dispatched to the midlands, where under the command of the governor, Suetonius Paulinus, they ultimately defeated Boudica. We are told that the legion from the south-west did not arrive and its commander committed suicide. Perhaps his soldiers were pinned down as they faced the last desperate rebellion by the Durotriges of Dorset and were unable to march north. But like so much in this story, this is far from certain.

3

DURNOVARIA AND THE ROMAN ADMINISTRATION

For the most part the Romans chose as their units of 'self-government' in Britain the native tribes as they existed before the invasion. Some had welcomed the Romans, and were rewarded with a special 'Client King' or 'Client Queen' status for their leaders. Among these were Cogidubnus in Sussex and Prasutagus in Norfolk. Others, who resisted strongly, were more harshly treated. But the privileged tribes lost their privileges when their original leader died, and all ended as normal *civitates* in the Roman province.

Each *civitas* had its capital, and in the case of the Durotriges this was to be *Durnovaria*, which we now call Dorchester (*17*). In terms of status the *civitas* capitals were the lowest grade of town in the province. Above them came the *municipia*, towns rewarded by the grant of Latin citizenship, an inferior form of Roman citizenship. Verulamium is the only known example. Above them were the *coloniae*, cities actually formed from Roman citizens. The first of these was Colchester, no doubt populated by veterans of Claudius' invading army. Later came Lincoln, Gloucester and York.

The Romans were very good at persuading conquered tribes to accept the Roman way of life and to acquiesce in Roman rule. It was more profitable than indefinite military control. One of the ways in which this was done was by retaining the nominal 'independence' of the local tribe and gaining the support of their leaders through formal recognition of their position and other benefits. Once possessed of beautiful villas, steam baths and the other trappings of Roman civilisation, the princes of the Durotriges were scarcely likely to lead a movement advocating a rebellious return to the windswept hilltop of Maiden Castle. It has even been suggested that the famous and magnificent Roman palace of Fishbourne, near Chichester, represents a direct reward to Cogidubnus, the pro-Roman chief of the Regnenses, and was used to entice the leaders of other tribes into Roman ways.

The word *civitas* is best left in Latin, as it means both the 'county' in geographical terms and the people themselves – a sort of 'county state'. A *civitas* needed a *civitas* capital, and this was to be Dorchester. All over Britain tribal governments were moved from the draughty hillforts (or wherever they had been moved to since the invasion) down to lower ground, and usually to take over now disused army camps to provide their first

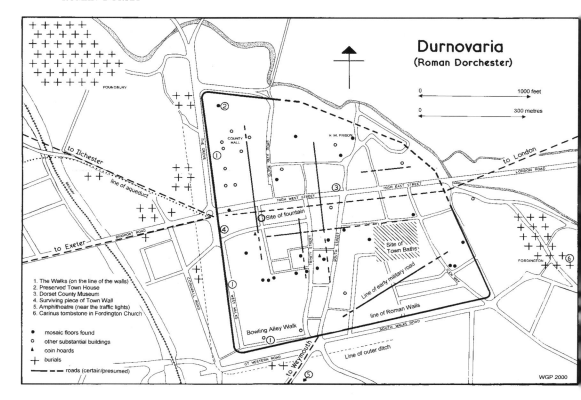

17 Map of Roman Dorchester

temporary buildings. As we have seen in chapter 2, something like this happened at Dorchester, though the original army camp has not been identified.

When did this occur? After the violence of the invasion, it will have taken some time. Nevertheless we know the general answer to this question. In the *Agricola*, which details the life of the governor of Britain from AD 77-84, Tacitus writes that he encouraged the building of temples, markets and houses. Those towns with reliable evidence for their beginnings, such as Cirencester, confirm that this was so. No doubt Dorchester was similar, though the evidence is not yet conclusive.

The governor may have appointed a *praefectus civitatis*, or civitas prefect, whose job was to advise the Durotrigian princes on the setting up of a Roman-style town as their capital, and a system of government in line with that of Roman towns throughout the Empire. No name can be put to a *praefectus civitatis* in Britain, but it is tempting to think that Carinus (see p.54), whose tombstone records his Roman citizenship so proudly at an early date in the history of Dorchester, could originally have arrived as the prefect and stayed to settle.

Though the governor provided encouragement and technical assistance (and no doubt compulsion if needed) the Durotriges had to pay for their own city. The Roman writer and philosopher Seneca is known to have lent millions of *sesterces* to British tribes to fund their Romanisation programme. The building of Dorchester must have been a financial strain. We do not know how soon elaborate and expensive public buildings appeared. The wealthy buildings we know of belong to the later third and the fourth century, but they must have had their timber predecessors in the first and second centuries.

Excavations in Dorchester in the last 50 years have made one thing very clear; the builders of Saxon and medieval Dorchester used the Roman buildings as a quarry on a systematic and, for the Roman archaeologist, devastating scale. Time and time again all that is found of Roman buildings are the empty foundation trenches. Not only has all the dressed stone and brick from the walls gone, but the foundations have been quarried away to the last flint.

In these circumstances it is difficult to offer reliable opinions on the appearance of the town at various stages of its Roman history, and particular importance attaches to the rare sites where substantial parts of Roman buildings have been found. These include the very well-preserved town house behind County Hall (now redisplayed), and the sequence of buildings found at 34 Trinity Street; these ranged from simple timber buildings in the first century, timber-framed buildings on stone foundations in the second, to a substantial stone and flint town house in the fourth. Peter Woodward's excavations in Greyhound Yard (Woodward 1993) provided another area of substantial urban buildings for study. Recently parts of another spectacular town house have been found during the conversion of the old hospital site in Princes Street to houses and flats (*28*).

Durnovaria is not a Latin word. We are lucky to know the name at all, as it occurs in only one ancient document, the *Antonine Itinerary* (a third-century route book). Most versions of the book actually spell it *Durnonovaria*, but one has *Durnovaria* and this is the name hallowed by use in modern times. No one is sure what it means, except that the first part may refer to fist-sized pebbles.

There is very little evidence on the site of Dorchester for pre-Roman settlement, though excavation on the old hospital site at Somerleigh Court did produce traces of Iron Age activity. There was probably a farm or even small village, which may well have been called *Durnovaria* in the Celtic language. The Romans rarely renamed places, and the new town will have been called after an existing site. It is just possible that *Durnovaria* was the name of Maiden Castle, and this was transferred to the new settlement, but there is no real evidence for this.

The gates and many public buildings must have carried monumental inscriptions recording the name and other valuable information but alas, not one has survived; the only inscriptions are on an altar dedicated by a legionary centurion (in Godmanstone church), the tombstone of Carinus (see below), a milestone and a stamped tile. None of these name the town or the tribe.

The nearness of Maiden Castle and the later history of the town strongly suggest that Dorchester was the Roman capital of the Durotriges, but surprisingly this cannot be proved beyond doubt. Nowhere in the *Antonine Itinerary* is the name of the tribe attached to the name of the town – *Durnovaria Durotrigum* – as was normally done with tribal capitals.

Curiously it is actually possible to prove that Ilchester (*Lindinis*) was a Durotrigian town. The stone from Chesters on Hadrian's Wall (*2*) that names the Durotriges says that they were from *Lindinis*. They were probably stonemasons from Ham Hill. On the basis of this inscription it has been argued that Ilchester became the capital of the Durotriges in the third or fourth century, or that it was of equal importance with Dorchester. However, it is easier to understand the inscription as simply specifying which working party was meant. There may have been another from Dorchester, presumably Portland stonemasons.

CITIZENSHIP

The citizens of *Durnovaria* had to be content with citizenship of their own tribe, the Durotriges. Full Roman citizenship was something very much coveted, in view of the privileges it brought. Everyone knows the story of St Paul, taken to Rome to a hearing before the emperor because of his citizenship. The only tombstone from *Durnovaria* itself records Carinus, a Roman citizen. The size of the letters indicates the importance of his citizenship.

There was one principal way of gaining Roman citizenship and that was by service in the army. The auxiliary regiments were formed from non-citizens, and after 25 years' service the reward was citizenship for the soldier and for his wife and children. No doubt Durotrigians would have been among the British regiments found serving in various parts of the Empire, though their name has not been found on inscriptions. However, soon after AD 200 the emperor Caracalla granted citizenship to all those within the Empire and this distinction became less important.

Not only were the inhabitants of Dorset citizens of their own *civitas*, but they were governed under native or Celtic law, not under Roman law. Celtic law was that of the native tribe as modified by the Roman government to match their own system. And on a capital charge a citizen had the right of appeal to the governor, in the same way as the Roman citizen could appeal to the emperor.

Everyday justice among the Durotriges was then more or less according to traditional Celtic law, and administered by Durotrigian judges. The governor went on circuit during the winter, when the armies were not campaigning, and no doubt from time to time the governor sat in judgement in *Durnovaria*. After the time of Agricola (AD 77-84) the appeal cases may well have been heard by the *legatus iuridicus*, a lawyer appointed to help the governor with his legal duties.

THE COUNCIL

The Durotriges were directly governed by a 'county' council, similar in functions to the modern one, but rather less democratic in its workings. This was called the *ordo* or the order. Its name and the names of its officers were similar to those of cities all over the Roman world.

Its members, theoretically 100, but usually fewer, were *decuriones*. These were the elders and nobles of the Durotrigian tribe, retaining their position of privilege. Membership depended on a property qualification. They became, at least on the surface, more fully Romanised than the rest of the people. They owned the rich town houses with elaborate mosaic floors; many also owned a rich country house or *villa*. Much of the trade and its profits were in their hands, as it had been before the conquest. We cannot, alas, put a name to a single one of them, unless one of them was a Paternus, who is named in a graffito on the wall of the preserved Roman town house. The nearest we can really get to them is to admire the mosaics which graced their living-room floors. For them the conquest meant a dramatic change in lifestyle, unlike the poorer people in the countryside.

The *ordo* made policy of its own accord in limited local areas of government, but more often interpreted centrally issued edicts of the governor or emperor. Perhaps in the last years of Roman Britain, as central government broke down, they came into their own, but we know little of it. The *ordo* will have met in the *basilica*, or town hall, adjacent to the *forum* or market place. We have no firm knowledge of these structures in *Durnovaria*, but it is worthy of note that an excavation on the site of Boots the chemist in South Street in 1971 found no trace of Roman buildings of any sort, the subsoil being entirely undisturbed. It is possible that the explanation for this is that this area is within the boundary of the *forum*. On this basis the *basilica* may well have been to the north and lie under the museum and St Peter's church.

THE MAGISTRATES

The chief executives of the town were known as the *Duoviri Iuridicundo*. *Duo* means two, and in accordance with Roman tradition of public office there were two of them, as of every other office. Either could veto the actions of the other. A curious system to our way of thinking, but designed to prevent abuse of office. For a similar reason the posts were annual. The *duovirs* administered local justice and presided at meetings of the *ordo* and the public assembly (*comitia*). They were responsible for public shows and the great religious festivals.

In addition there were two *aediles* or public works officers, who ran the roads, the drains and the water supply, and looked after public buildings. Two *quaestors* may have looked after local finances, but most taxation was collected by contractors on behalf of central government. Every fifth year a senior pair of magistrates were chosen to conduct the census, on which taxation was based. Theoretically all these magistrates were chosen by the people at the popular assembly in the market place (or perhaps in Maumbury Rings). But the *ordo* recommended candidates to the people and as the years passed the people's view became less and less important.

The prestige of office was great, but so were the expenses. If successful, you paid the bill for the election, and were expected to provide public entertainment, or build a temple or aqueduct or statue at your own expense. By the end of Roman Britain, citizens were reluctant to stand for office and compulsion was introduced. Many *decuriones* tried to move out of town to avoid it, something ultimately prohibited by decree.

THE PROVINCIAL COUNCIL

The *ordo* elected two representatives to the *concilium provinciae*, or provincial council, which met in London. At first sight this looks like a regional government advising the governor; but far from it. The governor was entirely autocratic and the provincial council met for formal purposes only, mainly connected with the imperial cult, the worship of the emperor.

Throughout the Empire the emperor was presented to the people as a god. It is doubtful if any one in Rome believed it, but it was used as policy among more primitive peoples as a means of ensuring obedience.

In the early years of the British province the council met at Colchester, where the foundations of the first temple of the imperial cult have been located under the Norman castle keep. This temple was the focus of the rebellion of Boudica in AD 60, and saw a dramatic siege and the death of everyone who had taken refuge there.

THE GOVERNOR

The governor kept his eye on what happened in *Durnovaria* through his own large civil service in London. The flow of paperwork from Dorset to London rivalled that of today, but none of it survives. The top men in the civil service were all seconded soldiers from the legions. Many grades of officials existed. In particular the *speculatores* (inspectors) travelled the province as personal representatives of the governor and will often have been in *Durnovaria*. All over the country you would have found *Beneficiarii* or 'beneficiaries', who were in positions of trust, running post stations, organising taxes and otherwise representing the governor's interests.

TAXATION

The benefits, if such they were, of Roman life, had to be paid for. Every five years the census detailed people and property, and taxation was based on this. The *Procurator Augusti Britanniae* was responsible for the finances of the province, and under him other procurators had smaller areas of responsibility. One procurator of Britain, Classicianus, achieved fame by bringing to an end the slaughter following the rebellion of Boudica. The procurator had a direct line of communication to the emperor, bypassing if necessary the provincial governor.

The Durotriges paid the three standard taxes to the tax contractors: the *annona*, or corn tax, to feed the army, the *tributum soli*, based on the productivity of the land, and the *tributum capitis* or poll tax. No doubt they paid up, reluctantly.

THE WALLS

Like most Roman towns in Britain *Durnovaria* was eventually walled, meaning defended by a fortification. At first this was a turf and timber structure of limited life, but later a stone face was added making it a much more permanent feature. The triangular outline of the walls can clearly be seen from the air (*19*). Walls and ditches covered a swathe over 100m wide. This has dominated the pattern of the town till Victorian times; not till then did the town spread outside (*18*).

The walls are best understood in the south-west corner in Bowling Alley Walk (see *15*). The wall stood on the edge of the grass verge. The bank which backed the wall (and contained the chalk from the ditches) extends across the path and some 20m into the former hospital grounds. The triple ditches extended further south, the outer, southernmost, one being under the far side of Great Western Road. Beyond that still, lay the counterscarp bank, now under the houses on the south of the road. The scale of the work was enormous.

The ruined walls were cleared and the Walks constructed in the early eighteenth century, fortunately for us making a permanent marker of their route. Their position is clear on the west, south and southern part of the east side. Only on the north is their route uncertain where the building of the castle and later the prison, and possible erosion by the river has made it impossible to know what happened. At a point just south of the Top o' Town roundabout a fragment of the stone wall survives (*20*). The facing stones have long since disappeared, but the core shows traces of the Roman style of building, with levelling courses of horizontal stones at intervals.

Imposing gates must have existed, on the west, south and east sides, but no trace has ever been found. Their positions can be calculated from the lines of the roads within

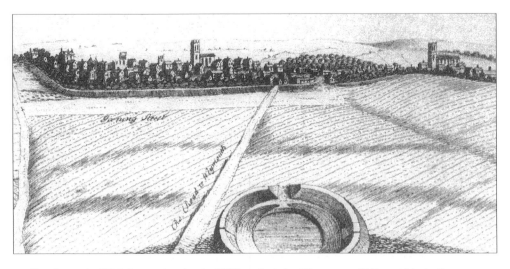

18 Dorchester in 1723 from a drawing by William Stukeley. The town still lies within its Roman walls, except for Fordington on the right-hand side

Left: 19 A vertical aerial photograph of Dorchester showing the line of the Roman walls

Below: 20 Fragment of the Roman town wall at Top o' Town, Dorchester

the town, which are known in part from excavation. The streets do not by any means correspond with the modern ones.

One might expect the walls of a Roman town to be rectangular, as were those of a fort. But a glance at plans of towns in Roman Britain shows this was not so and the reason is well understood. At first the towns, with one or two exceptions, did not have walls. Under the Roman peace (*pax Romana*) such things were unnecessary. Citizens were not allowed to carry arms. But, in AD 196, the governor Clodius Albinus did something later imitated by other governors of Britain. He declared himself Augustus and took the British legions to the continent to make himself emperor. Before he went, he took steps to make it possible for the province to survive attack in his absence. The essential feature of Roman life and control was the towns, and he gave orders for them to be defended by walls to protect themselves.

The towns then enclosed the areas that had already been built upon, in the case of Dorchester about 30ha (75 acres). This is the reason for the irregular shape of the town. It is interesting to imagine the meeting of the *ordo* at which military advisers came to discuss and plan the layout of the town walls. Discussions may have been fraught with problems. The wealthiest citizens who had built themselves town houses well away from the town centre may have found that military considerations precluded the inclusion of their house within the walled area.

An interesting discovery in excavations on the walls in Bowling Alley Walk (see *15*), was that prior to the erection of the earliest earth and timber rampart, a start had been made on the foundations of a stone wall. This had got no further, when the presumably urgent construction of a massive (but quicker) earth bank buried it.

The walls did not finally gain a stone face till some time in the third century. (The date for this is very uncertain, and the date for the original construction is not beyond doubt.) Many towns acquired bastions for artillery on the outer face of the walls in the fourth century. This may have happened at Dorchester, but there is no evidence for it.

MAUMBURY RINGS

Outside the town on the road to the harbour at Weymouth, lay the amphitheatre (*21*). Maumbury Rings is a far cry from the Colosseum in Rome, but its function was basically similar. We have already seen how it had a military use at first, but certainly it was adapted to use for the town at an early date. The Colosseum held over 50,000, while Maumbury Rings held about 5000.

It was entirely built of earth and timber, and never rebuilt in stone as the amphitheatre was for example at Silchester, tribal capital of the Atrebates. Perhaps Dorchester would never have had an amphitheatre had the military one not been to hand; certainly it was no longer used by the late second century. Whether Christians were fed to the lions there, or gladiators fell in combat, is doubtful. Such shows were expensive to put on, and the small town of *Durnovaria* may not have been able to support them. But some form

21 Maumbury Rings, the Roman amphitheatre

of entertainment must have occurred there, no doubt reminiscent of the modern circus. Perhaps these were a financial disaster and this lead to the abandonment.

However, just as the military amphitheatre will have enabled the commanding officer to address a whole legion, or conduct important religious and political ceremonies, so the later town will have used the Rings for such purposes. It will have been able to hold the likely free population of *Durnovaria*.

Maumbury Rings is one of the most remarkable ancient monuments of southern England. It is most famous as the amphitheatre of *Durnovaria*, but long before that it was first built as a henge monument in the Neolithic period, or New Stone Age. Much later, during the English Civil War of the seventeenth century, the Rings became a fortified outpost of Dorchester on the road to Weymouth and was held by the Parliamentarians. The nineteenth century saw public executions held there. Today musical events and festivals are held within the grassy banks.

As often with our ancient monuments, we are lucky that Maumbury Rings survives. In the 1850s the site escaped destruction at the hands of the new railway companies. The line of the Wiltshire, Somerset and Weymouth Railway passed close to the west. The connecting curve of the Southampton and Dorchester Railway would most conveniently have passed straight through the Rings, but a campaign led by William Barnes forced the railway to make the awkward sharp curve at Dorchester South Station to avoid it.

22 The Roman town house in Dorchester in 2005, showing the modern roof

THE TOWN HOUSE

It was almost certainly one of the native Durotrigian families which built and lived in the Roman town house in Colliton Park, behind the present-day County Hall. In view of the importance of this site and its availability for study (*22*), it is described here in some detail.

It has often been referred to as a *villa*, but this is incorrect as this term is reserved for country houses. In Latin it would have been called *domus*. Perhaps at one time it was called The House of Paternus (*Domus Paterni*), as there is evidence that someone called Paternus lived there.

The excavation

In 1935 Dorset County Council decided to construct a new County Hall in the north-west corner of the Roman town, in what had been the grounds of Colliton House. Very responsibly the opportunity was given to the Dorset Natural History and Archaeological Society to excavate this substantial area of the Roman town. This was organised by Lt. Col C.D. Drew who was then Secretary of the Society and Curator of Dorset County Museum.

There were two seasons of excavation, in 1937 and 1938, directed by Lt. Col C.D. Drew and K.C. Collingwood Selby. A number of archaeologists took part who were later to become famous, including Richard Atkinson and Graham Webster. The immediate results were published in the *Proceedings of the Dorset Natural History and Archaeological Society* (Drew & Collingwood Selby 1938 and 1939).

23 The excavation of the Roman town house in 1937. © *Dorset County Museum*

This was perhaps the first major urban rescue excavation in the country. The excavations uncovered the remains of at least six stone Roman buildings (*23*) which included several small three-roomed structures. There were also many other timber buildings. In addition there were pits, wells and various working areas. Building VII was interpreted as a smithy. It seems likely that some of the area was devoted to small-scale industry, as was later found in the garden of the old hospital in Princes Street.

However, the most spectacular find was Building I, closest to the north-west corner of the Roman ramparts and deeply buried. This was a substantial Roman town house in a surprisingly good state of preservation, when compared to the remains of other houses in the Roman town. It may be that the owner made his living from the industrial activity in this area. The location of the town walls in this corner may well have been decided in order to include the house, though it is not quite certain that the house was in existence at this time.

The decision was made not to build over this part of the site, and to preserve the house on permanent display. The outbreak of the Second World War followed swiftly on the excavations, and although the building of County Hall was completed (albeit to modified design), the full study and publication of the excavation was not achieved.

The development of the house

Although the results of the excavation were briefly published by the excavators and further discussed by the Royal Commission, full study of the data has never taken place. This description is based on the available information, but may in due course need revision.

A plan of the house appears in *Figure 24* and the reconstruction drawing by John Hodgson, shows how it might have looked late in the fourth century AD (*colour plate 10*). It is never possible to be quite certain of the appearance of a Roman house in Britain, but the drawing is based on a comparison with much better surviving houses in places such as Pompeii and Herculaneum, where the eruption of Mount Vesuvius in AD 79 buried many houses whole. Architectural styles were similar all over the Roman Empire.

Like all houses that were in existence for many years, it was not all built at once. It is possible to see in its foundations places where extra rooms and other features have been added. Coins are the most accurately datable type of archaeological find. Most coins from the site and much of the pottery belong to the period from AD 250-400, and this must be the main period of the building and use of the house.

Some finds belong to the second and early third century, and it may be then that the first buildings appeared. In many parts of the site there are traces of the postholes of wooden buildings which preceded the stone ones we see now. Several such postholes have been marked on the west side of Rooms 16 and 18 in the newly roofed part of the house. There were two separate ranges which never directly communicated except by way of the covered veranda. The south range includes Rooms 1-7 and the west range Rooms 8-18 (now covered by the modern roof).

The path shown on the plan approaching from the east is probably not Roman, but is later in date. The well in the courtyard is certainly Roman. One surprising discovery was

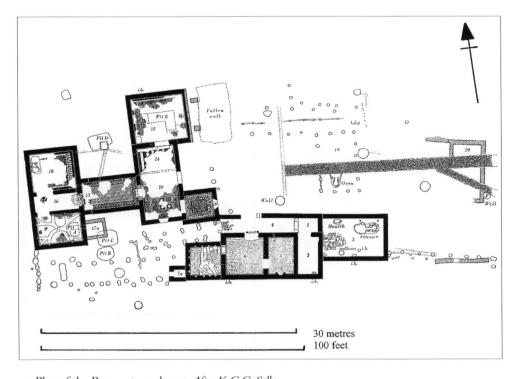

30 metres
100 feet

24 Plan of the Roman town house. *After K.C.C. Selby*

that at the end of the Roman period when the house had been abandoned, much debris from the walls and roof had been dumped in the well. Someone cleared the site, but it is not known when. The well was 10m (33ft) deep. The material in the well included eight short columns, which had probably stood along the veranda (Room 4). One of these has been re-erected on site, and two others and a column capital are on display in Dorset County Museum.

The stone and flint house had its foundations securely cut into solid chalk. The flints were roughly knapped and sometimes laid in herring-bone courses. Limestone slabs were used as quoins at the wall corners and for bonding courses. The flint came from almost anywhere on the chalk hills, and the limestone from Portland or possibly as close as the old quarries at Upwey.

None of these materials would have been visible in Roman times, as the walls were rendered inside and out. The outside was painted in Pompeian red, and the inside decorated in a variety of patterns, including geometric and floral designs above geometric panels. Substantial quantities of plaster fragments survive and future study may provide more detail about the schemes of decoration.

Some parts of the roof were covered with Purbeck limestone tiles, and the modern tiles used in the reconstructed roof over the remains are also from Purbeck quarries and cut to the Roman pattern. However, there are also many fragments of red clay tiles, and some rooms were covered in this material, certainly including Room 14 where many pieces were recovered from the filling of the well or fountain. The roof as recently reconstructed is at too steep an angle, as Roman roofs were normally at an angle of 20°. Many of the floors were made of mosaic, and these are evidence of the prosperity of the owners; the designs are characteristic of floors being laid in wealthy houses across Britain at this time (Cosh & Neal 2006).

The south range

The south range was a block of five main rooms (Rooms 2, 3, 5, 6 and 7) with a veranda along part of the north side (Room 4). Its history is not easy to understand, but it is the first stone building to be built on the site, and can only be understood in relation to the timber house, indicated only by its postholes, which continue the line to the west.

The likeliest explanation is that the story started with the timber house in the late second or early third century AD. To this was later added a heated living room (Room 7), with its stokehole (Room 7b) to the east. A hypocaust is a Roman system of under-floor heating with a stokehole on the outside of the building. Because of the fire risk it cannot be built of wood, so the new room was built in stone. This is the first sign of the developing luxury of the house. Other stone buildings were beginning to appear in the town about this time.

Then a small three-room stone house was built (Rooms 2, 3 and 6). This house continued to use the heated room and the stokehole had to be moved to the other side. The hypocaust was also completely rebuilt. At this stage all the floors were of *opus signinum* (crushed brick concrete). The wooden range may have continued in use for domestic purposes. Room 2 contained a small niche, which perhaps contained the statue of one of the gods worshipped by the family.

Finally Room 5 and the veranda were added. Room 5 had ovens in it, and may have been the kitchen. The veranda was built at a lower level and steps were needed to gain access to Room 6, where an *opus signinum* floor now covered the old stokehole. Because the new veranda was lower, it was necessary to underpin the north wall of Rooms 2 and 6 with the herring-bone pattern stone slabs which can still be seen.

The west range

About the middle of the fourth century, increased wealth enabled the owner to build the west range (Rooms 8–18) on a grander scale, eventually with elaborate mosaics in every room. Perhaps the site had been sold and had a new owner. The old south range remained in use; Room 5 was still the kitchen, and the nearby rooms were perhaps used for domestic purposes by the slaves.

The west range, easily identified now by its reconstructed roof, was built in several stages, though it is not possible to say how much time elapsed between the stages. The initial new construction seems to have involved Rooms 10, 13 and 14, though Room 13 was about 1m shorter at its west end than the final version. An interesting point is the provision of water channels between these rooms to enable the mosaic floors to be washed down. The channels led to a sump outside the building.

At the south end of Room 10 the excavators found the two jambs of a window fallen inwards. The window glass lay broken on the floor. This is the window which has been rebuilt on the site. Room 14 has what appears to be a well in the middle of the floor, cut through the mosaic. It has not been fully excavated, and there is still a possibility that it is a shallow ornamental pool, perhaps with a fountain, or even a well, built through the Roman floor at a much later date. The remaining rooms may have been added to the house all at once, or on separate occasions – it is not possible to tell. Room 8 was built in a position which linked it to the veranda of the south range. This is the only room in which the mosaic floor survives intact.

Room 15 was added beyond Room 14 on the north side. This is the largest room in the house with the finest mosaic, and was probably used as the *triclinium* (dining room). The mosaic replaced an earlier *opus signinum* floor. The high-quality mosaic has an outer border of black and white chevrons, with a wide inner swastika border enclosing rectangular panels of guilloche and chequers. Two circular medallions at the centre of the west and north sides contain respectively a female head with flowers which may represent Spring and a hooded head which may be Winter. The seasons were popular features of Roman mosaics.

When the site was derelict in the late fourth or early fifth century, the east and west walls of this room fell outwards, showing that they were at least 4.5m (15ft) high. Two stone bases suggest that buttresses had been needed to support the east wall, though it is also possible that there was an upper story with an outside staircase.

On the west side Room 13 was extended and a new floor laid, leading into three further new rooms, 16–18. It is not possible to be certain about the use of these rooms, except that Room 17 was heated by a channelled hypocaust with its stokehole on the east side (Room 17a). It was used as a winter living room, probably replacing Room 7, which was now awkwardly situated. It is interesting that the house had no private bath suite. The occupants must have used the public baths.

The finds

Many types of artefacts were found during the excavation. The most interesting ones are on display in Dorset County Museum's Archaeological Gallery, though the majority are in store.

A wide range of pottery was found, which together with the coins showed that the house in its main phase was in use in the late third and fourth centuries AD. This included fine table-ware from the potteries of the New Forest and of Oxford, and large quantities of black kitchen pottery (known to archaeologists as 'Black Burnished Ware'). This was made in Purbeck and traded widely in Britain, even as far as Hadrian's Wall (see chapter 10). Locally, Dorchester must have been one of the main markets, and this is where the pottery for the house was bought.

There were many small objects of bronze, iron, glass and bone. Perhaps the most amazing find was a chair or table leg in Room 17 (25). It came not from the house itself, but from a pit which was filled in at the time the house was built. It is made of Kimmeridge shale, an oily type of stone found in Purbeck which can be carved or turned on a lathe. A wide range of objects was made from the shale, and this chair leg is undoubtedly the most spectacular ever found. It was part of a very expensive piece of furniture.

A small clay stamp was found for marking pots of ointment. Its inscription means something like 'Yellow ointment for all running affections of the eyes'. One intriguing find was actually part of the structure of the house. In Room 17 many fragments of

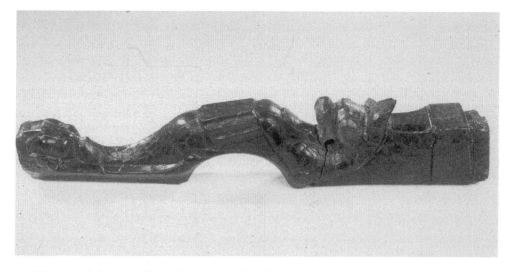

25 Table or chair leg made from Kimmeridge shale. © *Dorset County Museum*

26 Plaster fragment from the Roman town house with a *graffito* reading *Paternus scripsit* (Paternus wrote this). © *Dorset County Museum*

painted plaster from the walls were found in, having fallen into the channels of the hypocaust, the under-floor heating system. Among these was a fragment about 150mm (6in) long, which shows a *graffito* (*26*), or scribbled message, scratched into the plaster. It is repeated twice and says in Latin *Paternus scripsit*. This means 'Paternus wrote [this]'.

It is tempting to imagine a naughty child called Paternus scribbling on the wall when no one was looking! But this can hardly be the explanation, because it is written in the mature, educated handwriting of someone well used to writing. Perhaps it is a signature indicating authorship of some more extensive writing or drawing which appeared above it, but there were no other fragments to support this idea and why does it appear twice? It's very difficult to understand how it came to be where it is. Certainly someone in the house at one stage in its history was called Paternus. It may have been the owner.

There will have been many other houses in *Durnovaria*, and some have been glimpsed at various times and their mosaic pavements lifted or reburied (two have been installed in the floor of Dorset County Museum) (*27*). The recent redevelopment of the old Dorchester hospital site revealed substantial fragments of the floors of another large house, though little remained of its walls (*28*). Other houses will have been smaller and poorer and many artisans will have lived over their shops in crowded streets, though none of these have been excavated to date.

27 The Victorian Gallery of Dorset County Museum, showing Roman mosaics from the town displayed on the floor. © *Ted Flatters*

28 Recent discovery of the veranda of the Roman town house at Somerleigh Court, Dorchester

THE CEMETERIES

Around *Durnovaria* stretched the cemeteries, originally along the roads but later filling in considerable areas between them. Two areas have been extensively excavated; the Poundbury industrial estate and Fordington High Street.

At Poundbury excavations by Christopher Sparey Green over a number of years revealed over 1000 graves (*29*), their occupants rescued from the bulldozers constructing the industrial estate. A majority belonged to the fourth century AD, a time when the Roman Empire was officially Christian. They were buried on an east–west alignment and for the most part without grave goods. Family groups were in stone mausolea with paintings on the walls. Fragments of these give tantalising clues to the Christian ritual of the cemetery. The painted plaster is on display in Dorset County Museum (*colour plate 9*).

Most of the bodies were in wooden coffins, but the more important ones had lead linings, and a few were in hamstone coffins (*30*). Such coffins provide important evidence, as even hair may survive in such conditions. The bones from Poundbury have been analysed and published (Farwell & Molleson 1993), and give a substantial sample of the people of *Durnovaria* in the fourth century, with details of their size, appearance, diseases, and the other information which can now be obtained from such remains.

In Fordington most burials were excavated in Victorian times though there have been small excavations recently. Much of the hill on which the village lies was covered by the cemetery. Here there was a greater variety of burial, ranging from the Christian to flexed burials which, though dating to the fourth century, reflected the burial pattern of the native Durotriges (*31*). There were also cremations, common in the Roman world in the first two centuries AD.

Most interesting of all is the one and only inscribed tombstone from the town to be found, reused in the porch of St George's, Fordington. This stone, found in 1907, can still be seen in the church at the west end and there is a replica in Dorset County Museum (*32*). It is made of Purbeck marble, and would have been set in an ornamental surround and brightly painted.

It is the only tombstone surviving in Dorchester itself; there can hardly have been a large number, unless the cemeteries were stripped of the stones (as in London) to provide emergency building materials in the last years of Roman Britain. Even then, it is surprising that more have not been found somewhere. The stone belongs to the early years of the town, and must represent someone important. Unfortunately no indication is given of his function. The stone reads:

CARINO
CIVI·ROM
ANN·L
RUFINUS·ET
CARINA·ET
AVITA·FILI·EIUS
ET.ROMANA·UXOR

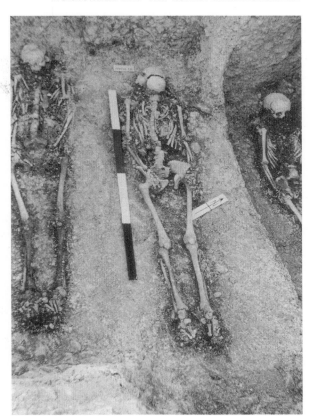

Right 29 Christian graves in the
Roman cemetery at Poundbury

Below: 30 A coffin made of
hamstone found in the cemetery at
Poundbury

31 Burial in the pagan Roman cemetery at Fordington. A Roman lady who died in childbirth is buried in the native Durotrigian style. Her baby is with her

32 The tombstone of Carinus from
Fordington

[In memory of] … Carinus, Roman citizen, [died] aged 50 years. His children, Rufinus,
Carina and Avita, with his wife Romana, [set up this memorial]

The first two names of Carinus have been lost from the top when the stone was exposed
to the frost. So we can put a name to these five inhabitants of earliest Dorchester. Clearly
Carinus' Roman citizenship was of the greatest importance. There would not have been
many such in *Durnovaria* in the first and second centuries. Maybe he was a citizen from
elsewhere in the Empire who was sent on government business, came to love Dorset
and stayed. He can hardly have been a Durotrigian native, as his name is not appropriate.
It is very tempting to think that he was *praefectus civitatis*, appointed by the governor to
guide the Romanisation of the Durotriges.

THE WOOL TOMBSTONE

There is one other inscribed tombstone from a site not far from Dorchester, which is
most conveniently discussed here (*33*).

A fragment of a Roman tombstone was found in the 1980s at New Buildings, Wool,
at approximately SY 838 856. The finder was Mark Vine of Weymouth. The location
is about 1km south-west of the village of Wool, in an area rich in Roman finds, first

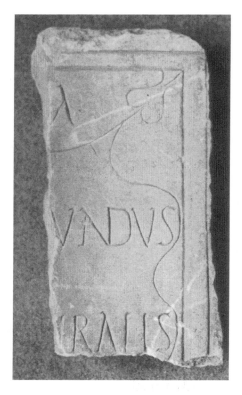

33 The tombstone from Wool

located at the time of the building of the nuclear power station at Winfrith, and in particular its pipeline to the sea. The deposits of Roman material are over 1m deep in places, suggesting a long-lived settlement site, whether villa, farm or even religious complex. Pottery at present on the surface dates from all centuries of the Roman period in Britain.

The stone from which the tombstone was made is a shelly upper Jurassic limestone, probably Portland rather than Purbeck, and perhaps from the Lulworth/Worbarrow area south of the find-spot. The fragment represents approximately one quarter of the original stone, cut square from the top right-hand corner. The present fragment measures *c.*21cm wide by *c.*40cm high, and the full stone will have been at least 40 x 80cm, perhaps a little more. In thickness it tapers from *c.*5cm at the top to *c.*6cm at the bottom. It has been deliberately cut to its present shape presumably for use in building work, and there will have been three other similarly sized pieces. Although the stone has been tumbled in ploughing, the inscription is well preserved.

An ivy-leaf decoration lies in the surviving corner, presumably matched by three at the other corners. These are joined by a wavy line enclosing the inscription. There is no direct parallel to this pattern in tombstones from Roman Britain. The letters are 8-9cm high, and are not in the formal style usual in inscriptions, but closer to the cursive style of handwritten letters. They are written along carefully drawn setting-out lines.

There are parts of three lines visible. The first line has the last part of an M, and undoubtedly read DM (*Dis Manibus*), showing that we are dealing with a tombstone. Although there is a wide gap between the lines, there is no evidence of further lines of letters in between.

The second line ends –VNDVS. This must be a cognomen, or nickname, and SECVNDVS, IVCVNDVS and VERECVNDVS are all possible. Tomlin and Hassall (Tomlin & Hassall 2000) prefer VERECVNDVS as they suggest this may have a Celtic name element within it. This identification is possible, as SECVNDVS and IVCVNDVS are probably too short to fill the full width of the stone. It is tempting to see this as evidence for a Romanised member of the Durotrigian upper classes, but this is far from certain. Verecundus simply means 'bashful', while Iucundus is 'delightful'. Secundus means 'fortunate' or perhaps just 'born second'.

The third line is more difficult. It certainly ends –RALIS. Before this there appears to be a letter I. However, in view of the cursive style of the lettering it might be an E, which is often written as II. If this is so, then there is only one real possibility, namely LIBERALIS. This is also a cognomen (meaning 'gracious' or possibly 'freeborn') and would mean that two individuals are commemorated, Verecundus and Liberalis, without the addition of their family and personal names. If this is the case, they might well be children, as Tomlin and Hassall suggest.

There is one other slight possibility for the third line, that the word is DUOVIRALIS, which would fit in length and accept the first surviving letter as I. This would mean that Verecundus had the rank of *Duovir*, i.e. he had at some time been chief magistrate of a town, presumably in this case Dorchester (*Durnovaria*). It is tempting to think that we have the tomb of one of the chief magistrates of Roman Dorchester, but this may be taking the evidence too far. The missing lower part of the stone will probably have given his/their age and date of death. The stone is the property of the Weld Estate, who have kindly allowed it to be displayed in Dorset County Museum.

THE AQUEDUCT

Roman Dorchester is perhaps most famous for its aqueduct, and this complex subject deserves a chapter to itself.

4

THE AQUEDUCT AND PUBLIC BATHS OF *DURNOVARIA*

For seven seasons from 1992-8 the author with the help of Iain Hewitt and Steve Burman studied the course of Dorchester's Roman Aqueduct from Poundbury to its source at the village of Frampton. The work was carried out with the assistance of students from various courses at Bournemouth University Department of Conservation Sciences, students of the HND in Practical Archaeology at Yeovil College and many volunteers.

As a result of this considerable effort the structure and history of the complex Dorchester Roman Aqueduct is now understood. It is the only Roman aqueduct in Britain to have been thoroughly examined.

PREVIOUS WORK

The first published study of the Dorchester Roman Aqueduct was that by Major J.U. Coates (Coates 1902). In a paper originally read in December 1900 he correctly identified the earthwork, which even as late as 1905 was curiously described as a Neolithic cattleway leading from Poundbury to Maiden Castle. The volume also provided additional material by W. Miles Barnes including, remarkably, a suggestion that there might have been a dam at Littlewood Farm.

Coates' map showed the line more or less accurately, following approximately the 300ft contour. In some places (e.g. Muckleford) he was apparently able to see lengths that have since been ploughed away. He placed the source of the water as the stream in Steppes Bottom, south of Frampton, close to the modern masonry dam near Foxlease Withybed. His work was remarkably accurate, though it was Miles Barnes who apparently spotted the true start point of the aqueduct at the dam at Littlewood Farm.

A later study of certain aspects of the aqueduct was made by Major Phillip Foster (Foster 1922). Two major alterations were suggested by him – first that the aqueduct continued further north-west to a source at Notton on the Frome, second that the channel was large enough to have served as a canal as well as a water supply. In his first suggestion of a continuation to Notton he was wrong, as the channel he saw was too low on the hillside to connect with the Roman work, and in any case was flowing towards the site of the Benedictine Priory at Frampton, to which it surely belonged. It is also very unlikely that a public water-supply aqueduct would have taken its water from a polluted main river. The suggestion that the channel was a canal, while interesting, can scarcely be true as the wide open channel only exists at the Dorchester end of the aqueduct, and there is no possible traffic for such a canal at Frampton.

The Royal Commission (RCHM 1970) unfortunately followed Major Foster's topographical account and agreed that the source was near Notton, though retaining the option of a source in Steppes Bottom. The Commission also referenced other work carried out on the aqueduct, including that by the Royal Engineers. The late R.A.H. Farrar, who did the work for the Commission, was always aware that the full story might not have been told.

TOPOGRAPHICAL DESCRIPTION

Like almost every other Roman town, *Durnovaria* had a public water supply for private consumers in houses like the town house described above, and particularly for the public baths excavated in 1977 in Icen Way. A water main made probably of oak logs has been found following one of the Roman streets towards the baths, though only the iron collars which joined the lengths survived. Somewhere near the old hospital site in Princes Street there would have been the *castellum divisiorum* or public fountain (*colour plate 7*), now celebrated by a small modern fountain on the site (*35*).

The aqueduct delivered water at approximately the level of the Top o' Town roundabout, after following the south-west side of the Frome Valley (*34*) from a source now confirmed to be the Steppes Bottom stream which joins the Frome at Frampton. At each re-entrant, rather than cross the low ground on overhead stone arcades as an aqueduct does, for instance, at the famous Pont du Gard at Nîmes, the Dorchester aqueduct detours up the re-entrant until the contour makes it possible for it to cross over to the other side, and then resumes its course along the Frome valley.

Close to Dorchester the channel has been excavated in recent times, notably by Christopher Sparey-Green in his work at Poundbury Industrial Estate (Green 1987). Beside Poundbury Hillfort, along the valley side to Whitfield Farm, and in and out of the Fordington Bottom re-entrant, the channel is clear to see on the surface (*36*).

Further north-west in the next re-entrant at Combe Bottom, although in favourable conditions the aqueduct can be seen as a soil-mark, its course is quite clear on the aerial photographs taken by John Boyden in the drought of 1976, and this has also been confirmed by excavation by AC Archaeology, appropriately on the line of the new Wessex Water main to supply Dorchester. Both these sources also demonstrate the presence of a smaller aqueduct just below the larger one.

The next re-entrant is at Bradford Peverell. There is little to see at present, although the channel has been excavated in the past and it has recently been visible in a pit cut in the yard of Home Barn Farm. Beyond this a long terrace runs through a young beech

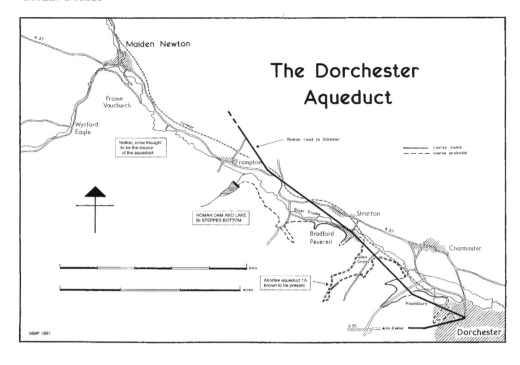

Above: 34 Map of the Dorchester Roman aqueduct

Left: 35 The water feature in Princes Street, Dorchester, commemorating the Roman aqueduct

Opposite: 36 The aqueduct terrace above the River Frome, west of the Dorchester, passing the Poundbury Iron Age hillfort. The terrace is just above the railway lines.

wood to a point nearly opposite Stratton Mill, followed by a small re-entrant called Green Valley, where the terrace follows its near-horizontal course till it enters Penn Wood and continues through the grounds of Quatre Bras.

North-west of Quatre Bras there is nothing visible on the surface anywhere in the Muckleford re-entrant, till the source is reached in Steppes Bottom at Littlewood Farm.

THE STRUCTURE OF THE AQUEDUCT

The two channels visible in the aerial photograph of 1976 turned out in the recent excavations to be three, the wider higher one concealing an earlier version (*37*). These have been labelled 1A, 1B and 2, since 1A and 1B were constructed probably in the same year, 1B being reworked by 2 at a much later date.

Aqueduct 1A

The first aqueduct was a failure. It ran below the line of the later, successful, 1B aqueduct, and was built from Dorchester as far as Bradford Peverell, but not as far as Green Valley where no trace of it could be found. No water ever flowed in the channel, which was

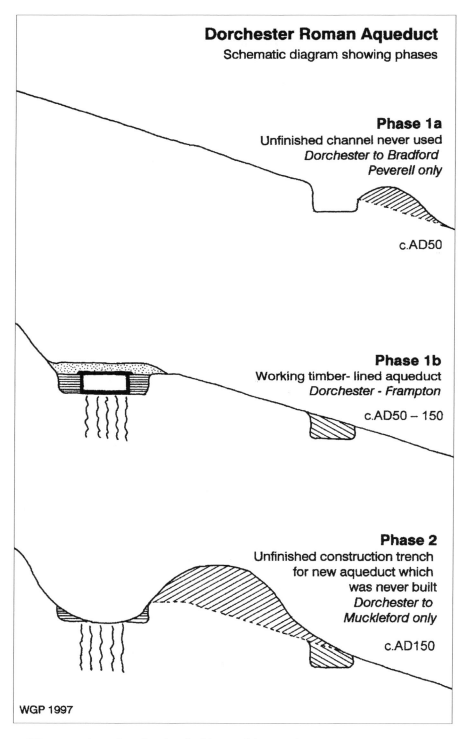

Dorchester Roman Aqueduct

Schematic diagram showing phases

Phase 1a
Unfinished channel never used
Dorchester to Bradford
Peverell only

c.AD50

Phase 1b
Working timber- lined aqueduct
Dorchester - Frampton

c.AD50 – 150

Phase 2
Unfinished construction trench
for new aqueduct which
was never built
Dorchester to
Muckleford only

c.AD150

WGP 1997

37 Diagrammatic sections showing the history of the aqueduct

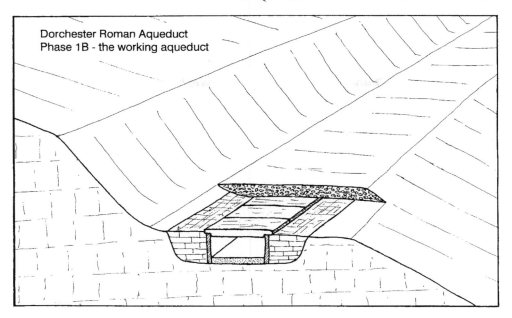

Dorchester Roman Aqueduct
Phase 1B - the working aqueduct

38 Diagram to show the construction of aqueduct 1B

filled with the material taken from it, shortly after construction and before soil had time to develop on its bottom. The gradient was very shallow indeed, and it would, if completed, have hit the Frome itself before it reached the stream at Steppes Bottom. It was abandoned, presumably because of inaccurate surveying, and refilled.

Aqueduct 1B

This was the only aqueduct that ever carried water. It was built of wood, as were the water mains fed from it in Dorchester. Cut into a terrace dug into the hillside, the channel had a waterproof clay bottom, timber sides and a timber cover (*38* and *colour plates 5* and *8*). Over this lay a shallow layer of soil to protect it from interference and from the weather and silt washing down the hillside. Interestingly the woodwork was self-supporting and not nailed together, making repair and replacement easy. The water channel itself measures about 80 x 30cm deep. There is no known parallel for this design.

The water was taken from the Steppes Bottom stream (originating at Compton Valence) at a point shortly before it entered the Frome at Frampton. By using the small stream rather than the Frome itself the engineers secured a supply of clean water. At Littlewood Farm the valley was dammed to form a lake, the function of which was to allow silt in the water to settle, and thus not block the underground channel. The lake was not a reservoir, as the aqueduct takes its water from the top level of the dam.

From here the channel ran gently downhill all the way to Dorchester at an average gradient of 1 in 1750, to deliver about 60l a second. The journey was 15km long, though as the crow flies it is only 7.5km.

Aqueduct 1B had never been seen before in excavation till the recent investigation, and this is because it only survives in the first mile from the dam towards Dorchester. This also explains why no surface features are visible at this end of the aqueduct's course. This aqueduct has been sectioned at Littlewood Farm close to the dam, at Higher Muckleford Farm, and at Dean's Computers close to Poundbury where one side of it survives.

Aqueduct 2

This is the apparently wide and open channel visible in Fordington Bottom and alongside Poundbury Hillfort. In places it has been smoothed by ploughing, but towards the top of the by-pass re-entrant it still shows what seems to be an open channel 3m wide and 1.5m deep.

This has been the cause of much confusion in the history of the study of the aqueduct. It appears to be a very large channel indeed, leading several writers to talk of a canal. This cannot however be the case, nor is it a water channel of any sort at all. It is not lined, and would not hold water in the friable subsoil of the upper chalk. It exists only from Dorchester to a point near Muckleford.

It is in fact a construction trench designed to facilitate the building of a new aqueduct to replace 1B. However, the actual aqueduct replacement was never built, and the construction work was abandoned before the dam was reached. The trench removed the existing aqueduct 1B, and this is demonstrated by traces of 1B in the bottom of aqueduct 2 in several sections, particularly one in Green Valley, and by the section at Dean's Computers where aqueduct 2 is slightly misaligned, allowing part of 1B to remain. This is shown in *Figure 39*.

Since the trench is so wide the intention was probably to build an aqueduct of stone or brick, after years of increasing maintenance problems with the timber one. There is ample clearance in the trench for workmen to carry out the task, but it is uncertain whether the job was ever started. The aqueduct has not been examined close to Dorchester itself, and this is where there might be traces if they exist. A good parallel is the Eifel aqueduct at Cologne, which is built of stone in a similar trench.

A large and presumably thatched building (see *41*) was found at Littlewood Farm, terraced into the hillside close to the dam. This probably represents the workshop and headquarters of the men engaged in the attempted reconstruction. It was also abandoned after a short period of use. It might be suggested that the intention was to replace 1B with a large open channel which was yet to be lined at the time of abandonment. But all Roman urban aqueducts are covered to ensure high quality of the water supply. Moreover one day's heavy rain would be enough to fill such a channel solid with silt if it were left open in this way along the steep and cultivated chalk hillsides.

THE AQUEDUCT BUILDERS

The biggest surprise in the aqueduct excavations was the discovery that beside the dam and lake at Frampton lay a small Roman fort, or more accurately a labour camp (*colour plate 6*), first discovered by aerial photography independently by Francesca Radcliffe and

39 A section across the aqueduct in the car park of Deane's Computers. On the right-hand side are traces of aqueduct 1B, not quite dug away by aqueduct 2 which is the main dark area

Mike Davis. The camp was heavily defended by a large V-shaped ditch (*40*) nearly 3m deep, with rampart to match. Its north-west gate lies only 20m from the dam itself. It lies in an unsuitable spot for a garrison fort, completely overlooked and on a steep slope. It can have had only one purpose – to protect men and equipment during the building of aqueducts 1A and 1B.

The interior contains only rainwater gullies presumably running between the lines of tents. From its south-east gate runs a metalled road (*colour plate 6*) heading for the now derelict quarries on the hill above Littlewood Farm, from which the materials for the dam came. This will have included chalk, flints and clay.

At the end of its usefulness, the camp ramparts were pushed back into the ditch and the site returned to agriculture. A native Durotrigian was later buried in the filled-in ditch, with fragments of pottery belonging to the first century AD.

The discovery that the hydraulic engineers of the Roman army built the aqueduct should not really have caused the surprise it did. The engineering and surveying skills needed are considerable, and not likely to be found outside the army. Even then, they seem to have made a mess of the first attempt (aqueduct 1A). A further consequence of this discovery is that the aqueduct was initially built not to serve the new Durotrigian town of *Durnovaria*, but rather the bath house of the Roman fort which undoubtedly existed near Dorchester (see chapter 2). This fort must have been substantial as the amphitheatre, Maumbury Rings, has also been shown to belong to the conquest period, and thus originally belonged to the fort.

40 The V-shaped ditch of the Roman labour camp at Littlewood Farm

Both aqueduct and amphitheatre were later converted for use by the civilian town, and the end of the aqueduct must have been realigned to enter the town rather than the fort. Direct proof of this remains to be found.

THE DAM

The remains of the dam still stand across part of the valley at Littlewood Farm 2.5m high. However, it is masked by the silt of the lake on one side, and the material from its own collapse on the other, leaving only about 0.5m visible. This is why it has not been noticed before, though it is possible that W. Miles Barnes spotted it in 1900.

A machine section was cut across the dam, though it was too dangerous to enter and record fully. The core of the dam was made of puddled chalk and crushed flint. The water face was clay. The level of the aqueduct shows that the dam was 6-7m high and the buried soil beneath the aqueduct core was covered in brushwood charcoal, presumably from the clearance of the site before construction. The spot at which the aqueduct entered the lake had unfortunately been removed by a medieval hollow way.

There can be no doubt that at some point in its history the dam collapsed, but there is no proof of the date at which this happened. The maintenance of earth dams requires expert attention, especially in the need to keep the earth core drained. It is tempting to think that it was the collapse of the badly maintained dam that brought the attempted reconstruction of aqueduct 2 to a disastrous end.

THE LABOUR CAMP

The labour camp measures approximately 45 x 80m. Only the south-west half was examined. It has been much damaged by the traffic on the medieval hollow way, which has probably destroyed both gates. Test trenches in the interior yielded only rainwater gullies, presumably to stop flooding of the tents.

The V-shaped ditch measured a little over 2m deep and 3.5m wide (*40*), but in view of the extensive ploughing of the field in the Middle Ages (the furlong strips are visible in *colour plate 6*) it may have originally been as much as 3m deep. All this material was built into the rampart, which must have been very substantial. After a short time the rampart was pushed back into the ditch when the project had been completed. A good parallel is the labour camp at Chew Green on Dere Street, built for the construction of the fortlet there, though this example was not demolished after use.

THE PRIORY LEAT

Major Foster's map of 1922 and the RCHM map of 1970 show a water channel on the north-west side of the Steppes Bottom stream. As no accurate level for the Roman aqueduct was available at that time, it was assumed that this was part of the Roman aqueduct. However, levelling and excavation of this channel shows it to be heading downhill towards Frampton House, not towards Dorchester. It is 1.5m below the level of the Roman aqueduct on the opposite side of the valley and it seems likely that it is the water supply for the Benedictine Priory which formerly occupied the site of Frampton House.

THE DATING OF THE AQUEDUCT

The discovery of the labour camp at the dam site at Littlewood Farm in Frampton makes it clear that aqueducts 1A and 1B belong to the conquest period, when the army was resident in the fort at Dorchester. Though neither the fort nor its bath house have been found, there is ample evidence that they must have existed. Durotrigian pottery found in the Littlewood camp ditch parallels that found in Wheeler's 'war cemetery' at Maiden Castle. This pottery continues in use throughout the first century AD, but the military context makes it almost certain that the aqueduct belongs to about AD 50, when the fort at Dorchester and the road network were firmly established.

It is possible to put forward a date for the attempted reconstruction of aqueduct 2 at two sites. One is the 'workshop' (*41*) excavated at Littlewood Farm on the same spot as the camp, which contained samian ware and appropriate coarseware of the mid-second century AD. The second site is the overflow channel behind County Hall in Dorchester, excavated in 1937-8 during the work on County Hall, and again by Jo Draper in 1968 (Draper & Chaplin 1982). This channel belongs of course to the later stage of aqueduct

41 The 'workshop' at Littlewood Farm

1B, when it had been diverted into the new town. Both excavations concluded that the channel was derelict by the middle of the second century AD.

As the attempted reconstruction of aqueduct 2 was disastrously abandoned, this means that this was the end of the life of the aqueduct, surprisingly early in the history of the town. However, this is paralleled by the amphitheatre, Maumbury Rings, similarly abandoned by that date or soon after.

In the 1937 excavation of the overflow channel a coin of Vespasian was found sealed in the lining. This, though only providing a *terminus post quem*, fits well with the probable date of the founding of the town itself and the consequent diversion of the aqueduct.

THE PUBLIC BATHS AT *DURNOVARIA*

These lay in the south-eastern part of *Durnovaria*, and were excavated in part in 1977 by David Bachelor (*colour plate 2*). They are briefly reported in the *Proceedings*, vol.99 for 1977, p.121 and vol.100 for 1978, p.114. At the time of writing publication of a full report is expected shortly.

For a small Roman town they are very large (*colour plate 3*), and confirm that upper-class Durotrigian society in *Durnovaria* adopted all the social features of life in the Roman Empire at large. They appear from the preliminary assessment of the excavation results (*42*) to have continued in use till late in the fourth century AD. This of course presents a problem, as by this time the aqueduct was long out of use. Was an alternative

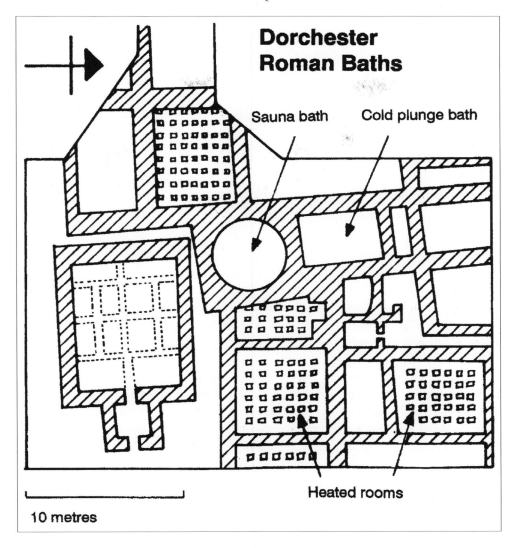

Dorchester Roman Baths

Sauna bath

Cold plunge bath

Heated rooms

10 metres

42 Plan of the excavated portion of the Roman baths at Dorchester

water supply found? Perhaps a bucket–well? Or could it be that the buildings were still in use in the third and fourth centuries, but not as baths?

It is tempting to speculate that the site of the baths of *Durnovaria* was also the site of the fort baths, and that the earliest phase of construction belongs to the military conquest. There is however no firm evidence for this theory.

5

LINDINIS (ILCHESTER) AND *VINDOCLADIA* (BADBURY)

LINDINIS (ILCHESTER)

Ilchester is of course in Somerset today. Nevertheless it is quite clear that the Roman town lay in the territory of the Durotriges. The inscriptions from Hadrian's Wall, presumably left by parties of Durotrigian stonemasons (2), name both the tribe and the town of *Lindinis*. Curiously we can be more certain about the status of Ilchester than we can of Dorchester.

It has been suggested that late in the history of Roman Britain either Ilchester replaced Dorchester as the *civitas* capital of the Durotriges or that the tribe was divided into two *civitates*. The present author sees no need for such reorganisation. The stonemasons were proud of their work, and simply recorded their tribal name and the town they came from. No doubt there were other lost stones which named the Durotriges from Dorchester. The Ilchester men surely worked in the extensive quarries on Ham Hill.

The origin of the Roman town at Ilchester lies in the presence in Iron Age times of a substantial embanked enclosure (43) on flat ground in the meadows just south of the later town. It may well have been called *Lindinis*. We have very little knowledge of this site and its function. There has been no major excavation. However, it probably represents a Late Iron Age development away from the old hillforts (in this case Ham Hill) to a lowland town more convenient for trade and life in general. It had a single rampart and ditch.

The Roman army arrived here early in the conquest and constructed a fort at the point where their major road, the Fosse Way, crossed the River Yeo. Ilchester lies on a small island of gravel within the Yeo's floodplain. The Fosse Way gave access to Lincoln via Bath and Cirencester in a north-easterly direction, and eventually to Exeter and the Second Augustan Legion's fortress to the south-west. It has even been suggested that the Fosse Way was intended to be the frontier of the new province, but if this was the case, the idea was soon abandoned, under pressure from the Silures of South Wales.

The evidence for this early fort is slight at the present time, consisting of cropmarks on the north bank of the river. At an early stage the road to Dorchester was built to provide a connection to the south-east.

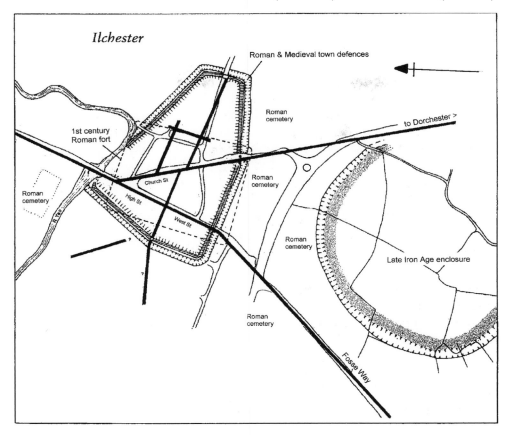

43 Map of *Lindinis*, the Roman town of Ilchester. © *Peter Leach*

At a slightly later date a larger fort was built, of which we have a little more knowledge. It covered about 7ha, and the later civilian town lay directly over it. The Fosse Way appears to have passed through the fort. The line of all four sides have been located, and some details of its defences are known. Seven hectares is a substantial area, and is enough to have contained several legionary cohorts and an auxiliary regiment, though we have no detailed knowledge of this.

In addition to the fort itself some buildings of timber are known along the Fosse Way to the south-west and these represent the first development of the *vicus*, or civil settlement. Most Roman forts in Britain of any permanence had a *vicus*, where local people arrived to trade with the soldiers. In many cases the *vicus* continued to develop into a town after the army had left. No doubt this also occurred at Dorchester, but details of the fort there are unknown (see chapter 3).

It may be that the building of such a substantial fort at Ilchester may have been a response to the Boudican rebellion of AD 60, when the Second Augustan Legion failed to arrive in the midlands to face Boudica, presumably because of unrest in the south-west. We have already seen the possibility that the violent action in the south-west gate of South Cadbury Castle was connected with these events. Pottery and coins suggest that the large Ilchester fort was built at this time. In the AD 70s the army left the south-west, and as at Dorchester the building of a Roman style town began; development was substantial by the end of the century.

The Roman town of Ilchester lay within a particularly wealthy region, a wealth based on agriculture and some industry such as the stone quarries on Ham Hill. This was reflected in the later Roman period by the number of luxurious villas in the area. The economic situation is however complicated by the possibility that some of the wealthy villa owners were incomers from the provinces of Gaul, attracted by a town and countryside well removed from barbarian attacks in the third and fourth centuries. The owners of the villas will have also been *decuriones* on the town council (the *ordo*) of *Lindinis*.

Recent research by the *Time Team* and others continues to find new villa sites in the Ilchester area, including Dinnington and Lopen. There is a contrast between the villas of Ilchester and those of Dorchester. Far more are known around Ilchester (about 35) than around Dorchester (about 15). To some extent this may reflect the intensity of archaeological research, but it seems inescapable that Ilchester was the place to be in the later part of the Roman period. It is difficult to be sure of the reasons for this. What did the citizens of Ilchester (*Lindinienses*) think of the citizens of Dorchester (*Durnovarienses*)? We can only speculate.

Although Ilchester was one of the smallest towns of Roman Britain, the villas in particular suggest that it was a thriving and prosperous community. Clearly Ilchester was an important market centre. From the surrounding countryside farmers and villagers will have come to market, as will the wealthier landowners and their families, bringing their produce to sell and to buy goods such as wine, oils, clothing, ornaments and jewellery, tools and implements, and pottery and glass, as well as to pay their taxes. Within the town, shops and workshops would have been busy supplying both their fellow townsfolk and visitors, some of whom would have come from further afield.

As in Dorchester, archaeological research in the Roman town has been piecemeal, and no major area has been cleared and redeveloped. The main roads intersect in the town, and there are traces of the expected street grid. The roads were surfaced with gravel, and show several phases of resurfacing. Complete building plans are rarely found. There have been about 30 finds of mosaic floors within the town (particularly that in a building complex at Ivel House). As might be expected, stone buildings were usually constructed of hamstone from Ham Hill, as is still the case with many buildings from recent centuries.

The town covered approximately 10ha (as compared with Dorchester's 30ha). The walls were built perhaps late in the second century, but extensive suburbs existed outside the walled area, particularly across the river to the north and along the Fosse Way to the south-west. It is interesting that the town apparently expanded beyond the walled area, indicating continued prosperity, something that did not happen at Dorchester as far as is known. But it may simply be that the walled area at Dorchester was so much larger.

Ilchester has provided one example of premises of a small shop on a street corner, with a shop, workshop and living room. Many such establishments must have existed both in Ilchester and Dorchester.

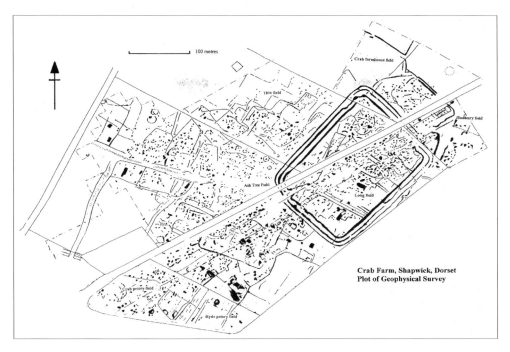

44 Map of the newly discovered town of *Vindocladia* near Badbury Rings. © *Martin Papworth*

So far no trace had been found of major public buildings such as the *basilica* and *forum*. They may yet appear, but it is also possible that if Ilchester was simply a small country town and not a *civitas* capital, they may not have existed. Nothing is known of an amphitheatre or baths, but it is likely that these will have existed at least for the fort, and probably for the later town.

A substantial cemetery has been found at Northover, beyond the Roman suburbs. Accidental discoveries and some excavation suggests that over 1500 of Ilchester's citizens were buried here. The graves echo those of the Dorchester cemeteries (see chapter 3). Many were buried in wooden coffins, but some of the town's wealthier inhabitants could afford lead or stone coffins, and possibly mausolea. Most of the burials belong to the fourth century, although the cemetery could have a much earlier origin.

The end of Roman Ilchester is as little understood as that of Dorchester. Its wealthy citizens will have increasingly taken refuge within the walls of the town for protection, but as the whole economic structure of the province collapsed in the early fifth century, the Roman way of life will gradually have come to an end.

VINDOCLADIA (CRAB FARM, SHAPWICK)

In 1976 the late Norman Field published what was thought at the time to be a small Roman auxiliary fort on Crab Farm, Shapwick, lying across the Roman road from the

Badbury Rings junction to Dorchester (see chapter 11). This Shapwick should not be confused with the Shapwick which lies in the Somerset Levels. The name simply means 'sheep farm'.

This site is on National Trust land, and subsequent research by Martin Papworth on their behalf has produced a most unexpected outcome. The fortified area (*44*) was the presumed fort or citadel in the centre of a substantial unwalled town, with a long history going back into the Iron Age.

It was not a planned town with a street grid, but developed piecemeal on a commercial basis, rather like the Roman settlement at Charterhouse in the Mendips, which grew up around the lead mines.

The Crab Farm site covers an area, yet to be fully defined, but exceeding 25ha. It lies on the north-east edge of the modern village of Shapwick (ST 945 022) and extends for over 700m to the edge of a scarp that slopes down to Crab Farmhouse. From the scarp edge there is a clear view of Badbury Rings hillfort which lies 2km further north-east. This large settlement may well be the site of Roman *Vindocladia*, a place mentioned in the *Antonine Itinerary* as lying on the road linking *Sorviodunum* (Old Sarum) with *Durnovaria* (Dorchester). This had long been thought to refer in some way to Badbury itself, but the new site recently found provides a much more convincing location for the name. Its prime position between the River Stour and the Roman crossroads north of Badbury enabled the settlement to develop into a significant local centre.

The site has archaeological features starting in the Early Bronze Age. The earliest remains are ring ditches, which probably represent ploughed-out burial mounds. A linear bank and ditch has been dated to the Middle to Late Bronze Age and geophysical survey indicates that it was reused as a boundary when an Iron Age settlement was enclosed on the crest of the scarp.

The Iron Age settlement covered over 2ha and Middle and Late Iron Age pottery has been recovered from the site. After the Roman conquest, the site continued to be occupied and at some time in the second or third century a triple-ditched fortification was constructed that enclosed about 3ha (*45*). The fortification was built over the south-west half of the Iron Age and Roman settlement. Its construction reflects the importance of the town in the later part of the history of Roman Britain, and the need to protect what may have been a *mansio* or posting station, an essential element in government communication and control.

Around and within the fortification, rectilinear enclosures and trackways follow a similar alignment to the fort, but it is likely that the Romano-British settlement flourished before the fortification was constructed. A puzzling feature of the excavations is that the Roman road from Badbury Rings to Dorchester appears to lie over various features of the Crab Farm site, suggesting that the road was built late in the Roman period. This cannot however be the case, as the road is clearly of early military date both at the Badbury junction and at its point of arrival in Dorchester itself. This puzzle remains to be resolved. South-west of the survey area, the route of the road is still the High Street of the village of Shapwick, thus indicating the continuous use of this section of the road for a very long period.

45 Excavation at *Vindocladia* of the inner ditch of the fortified citadel

It is likely that further Romano-British building remains would be found under the present houses and gardens of the village. During the Roman period, the settlement probably expanded south-west towards the river, and for economic reasons it would be important to construct buildings along the Roman road, particularly at the river bank where the road fords the Stour. Shapwick is mentioned in Domesday Book and it seems likely that, although reduced in size and importance, the settlement as well as the road would have continued to be used after the Roman period. Therefore, it is likely that the modern village is a direct descendant of the Iron Age settlement.

This investigation is one of the most significant pieces of research currently in progress in Roman Dorset.

6

THE COUNTRYSIDE

Historians once used to imagine the Romano-British countryside as some sort of idyllic parkland with a splendid villa glimpsed through the trees every few miles. It is now realised that in the later years of Roman Britain the population had almost certainly risen to a level which was only to be reached again at the time of the Industrial Revolution. In fact one of the most tragic results of the end of Roman Britain is that the population dropped to a fraction of its former number; a process that almost certainly involved a great deal of misery and suffering.

It is very difficult to calculate populations at remote periods in history. The Romans held a regular census of course, but the records do not survive. The only way to achieve an estimate is to look at two things; the size and number of towns, and any countryside areas where we have a complete sample of the population density.

In some areas of the fenland in Lincolnshire, aerial photography has shown that newly settled land maintained small settlements at intervals of less than 1km. Nearer Dorset, the route of the M5 was carefully studied in advance of the building of the motorway, giving a linear sample across Gloucestershire and Somerset. As in Lincolnshire Roman settlements were found to exist much more frequently than had been imagined. In many parts of the country which are sparsely inhabited today, such as the chalk downs in Wessex, settlements abounded. The result is a current estimate of population of over 5 million, a considerable increase on a probable Iron Age population of 1 million.

What caused this population explosion? Farming methods were improved to some extent by the introduction of Roman technology, though this is one of the most difficult topics to investigate. More importantly there was a large military and civil market for food which encouraged (or rather demanded) an increase in production. Finally, and most significant of all, the *pax Romana*, or Roman peace, meant that many generations lived their lives in peace without regular warfare to reduce their numbers and ruin agriculture.

As the numbers increased, new settlements sprang up and more and more land was taken into cultivation. In the fens of eastern England Roman water engineering made possible the draining and reclamation of large areas of land which were then intensively settled. In Dorset it is doubtful whether any substantial tract of land remained unsettled.

In fact the supply of timber for fuel and construction work must have been a major problem for the Durotrigian administrators.

Settlement in Dorset was enormously varied. There were the villas occupying the choicest positions and some of the best land. There were farms, large and small, of less than villa status. There were hamlets consisting of several farms grouped together. There were small villages and large villages. In fact, a similar variety of settlement existed to that of today with a much larger percentage of the population living in the country.

The formal changes brought about by the Romans centred mainly on the towns. Only gradually did the effects reach the countryside. A Durotrigian farmer continued to live as his ancestors had; his house was round, built of timber and thatched. His fields were small, the size that could be ploughed in a day. (His fields can still be seen in many places – they are referred to by archaeologists as 'Celtic' fields.)

He grew spelt (a primitive form of wheat), and kept the usual domesticated animals; sheep, goats, pigs and cattle. At all times and places in Roman Britain mixed farming was the rule, as it has continued to be until very recent times.

Gradually changes came about. The pottery bought in Dorchester changed shape because it was primarily made for the military market. The farmer could buy more of it, as the new towns and the army provided a profitable market for his produce even after taxation. New crops were introduced, including rye, oats, vetch and flax. In addition there was cabbage, parsnip, turnip, carrot and other vegetables. In favourable areas fruit trees were grown including the vine, plum, apple, mulberry and walnut. Wine was the Roman drink, but it never entirely replaced beer drinking in Britain. Wine must have been made in Dorset but, as now, found it difficult to compete with wine from more favourable growing areas on the continent.

The farmer's house might have stayed as it was; round huts are found throughout Roman Britain. But where Roman influence was stronger and more money became available, houses were gradually rebuilt in Roman style. The critical change was to a rectangular shape, and with it came tiled roofs and painted and plastered walls.

The best-known Roman village site in Dorset is Meriden Down near Winterbourne Houghton. Like many such villages it lies not in the valley with the later medieval villages, but on a chalk spur of comparatively high ground. It occupies nearly 2ha. Like a deserted medieval village it includes platforms representing ruined houses (some rectangular, some circular), working areas and small enclosures. Interestingly, the houses lie centrally in an area cut off by fences from the surrounding fields. Rather than the houses surrounding the village green, the green surrounds the houses.

But other villages are different and every imaginable shape occurs, including long streets with houses either side, and houses clustered round what looks almost like a village green. The villages which survive unploughed as earthworks are rare and valuable. Meriden Down and Grimstone Down (near Dorchester) and a few others hold many secrets of the Dorset countryside in Roman times and deserve major and intensive investigation. In the meantime they must be protected from damage as carefully as more spectacular monuments.

At Grimstone Down (46) the village lies at the top of the hill in the background of the aerial photograph. There has been no excavation, but pottery from molehills dates from

46 The Iron Age and Romano-British village on Grimstone Down, near Dorchester. © *Francesca Radcliffe*

47 The Romano-British farm on Ringmoor, near Turnworth in north Dorset

the Iron Age to New Forest Ware manufactured in the fourth century AD. The village may have had a life of a thousand years.

A lane can be seen running from the village, down the hill towards the camera, making a right-angled turn and leaving the area of cultivated fields to provide access to the mostly forested ground in the valley on the left. The lane enabled animals – perhaps pigs – to be driven to forage in the woods without them straying into the cultivated fields on either side. The small banks which mark the margins of the fields must have carried hedges or fences.

The pattern of the fields is not a neat checkerboard of regular shapes. Rather, each field seems to have been added to the pattern piecemeal as a new family set up home or there were more mouths to feed. At least 30 fields are visible in the unploughed part of the village, which is a scheduled ancient monument. In the upper left part of the photograph faint marks can be seen showing fields outside the scheduled area, which have largely been ploughed away. Interestingly these seem to be in a regular rectangular pattern. It is tempting to see these as having been added during the Roman period when such a job would involve the *agrimensores*, the land surveyors.

Another Dorset example of an Iron Age/Roman agricultural landscape is at Turnworth near Winterbourne Houghton. It is usually known as Ringmoor. Again by an accident of history a substantial piece of the ancient landscape has remained unploughed in modern times (47). This time a single farm is visible in the centre of the photograph, enclosed in a circular bank and ditch. Outside the ditch is an open area, from which two lanes set off between the fields.

One of the few excavated hamlets is at Studland on Poole Harbour. Here buildings dated from the conquest to the end of the Roman period. Round huts were succeeded on the same sites by roughly rectangular huts measuring about 12 x 7m. These were still of wattle and daub, but had substantial stone foundations. They were rebuilt many times, but basically were 'long houses' where the family lived in one end and the animals in the other. This was the form of the original farm building at the Dewlish Villa site, but there further development took place.

One of the excavations carried out by the great Dorset archaeologist General Pitt Rivers, was at Iwerne Minster (48). This took place in 1897, near Park House Farm Buildings. It provides a valuable story of the development of a small farm from its Iron Age origins to a very modest Roman villa.

The site is on Upper Greensand, about 70m above sea level, on a gentle rise in the low-lying ground at the headwaters of the River Iwerne; from south and east it is overlooked by the higher ground of the escarpment.

The Iron Age settlement is represented by numerous pits. From it came Durotrigian silver coins, a La Tène I bronze brooch, a bronze belt-link and a bone weaving comb. In Early Roman times the settlement was modified by the digging of ditches and sub-rectangular pits; finds of this period included coins dating from the reign of Vespasian to Commodus, brooches, and samian pottery of the first and second centuries. No house-site was found, but there were suggestions that the centre of occupation lay north-west of the excavated area.

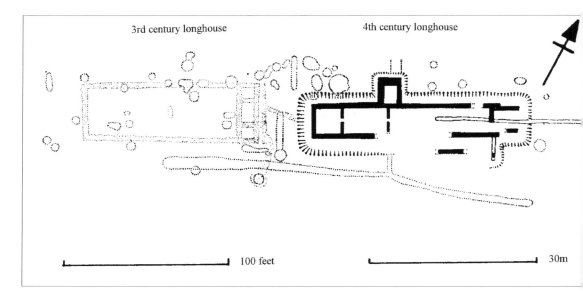

48 Plan of the small Romano-British farm at Iwerne Minster. *After RCHM*

During the third century a building, nearly rectangular in plan, 112 x 39ft, with flint footings 3ft wide, occupied the western part of the site. The north-east end of the building was divided into three rooms, 8ft in length and respectively 7ft, 13ft and 8ft in width. The entrance was probably on the north-east, where postholes for a porch were found. The rest of the building, with a pit or posthole at the centre measuring 8 x 2.5ft wide x 6ft deep, was partly flint-paved; it has been suggested that it was an aisled barn, although no holes or bases for aisle-posts were noted. Coins ranging in date from Gordian I to Tacitus were found in or near the building.

Lastly, *c.*AD 300, a substantial building was erected on an oblong site levelled into the rising ground on the east, some 25ft away from the building described above; it measures 126 x 18ft and the walls, of flint rubble, 2.5-3.5ft in thickness, remain standing in places to a height of 6ft. The main range is divided into four compartments and a fifth room, 16ft square, projects from the north-west side. A corridor or out-building lay along the south-east side. The compartment at the north-east end, 15ft long, may have been a porch. The adjacent room, 64ft long, was probably a cattle-shed since a stone-filled drain 2ft wide extended down the centre of the range from a point 28ft from the south-west end of the room; a quern was found *in situ* near the middle of the western part of the room. Next on the south-west is a room 27ft long, roughly paved, and communicating by axial doorways 2ft wide with the rooms to north-east and south-west. The south-west room is paved with small slabs of Kimmeridge shale and its walls, except on the north-east, are lined with plaster, painted with rectangular panels above a broad dado-line. The fifth room, on the north-west, has doubled walls, the inner of which, only 4ft high, probably carried a floor; this is likely to have been a granary. Coins ranging from Maximian to Decentius as well as New Forest Ware and coarse pottery, found during the excavations, indicate occupation of the building until *c.*AD 360.

Some idea of the agricultural processes of Romano-British farms can be obtained by reading the works of two Roman authors on farming. Both Columella and Varro describe in detail the farming year for all sorts of crops and animals. One thing is abundantly clear – it was very hard work.

The only type of plough that was available, both in the Iron Age and the Roman period, was the ard. This was simply a wooden spike that was dragged through the soil, usually by a pair of oxen. The only change that the Romans brought about was to provide an iron tip for the spike and a coulter or vertical knife to cut the sod and help the ard through the soil. The ard simply broke up the ground. The weeds remained on the surface. It was usual to plough in two directions, if not four. After this it was necessary to go over the ground removing the weeds by hand. It took at least nine operations to get a crop sown. The invention of the mouldboard plough which turns the sod and buries the weeds was one of the great inventions of the Saxons.

Some other agricultural hand tools were introduced, including the scythe. There is some evidence, both in literature and sculpture, of an extraordinary mechanised harvesting machine called the *vallus*, but little if any evidence for its presence in Roman Britain. It was probably just an ingenious curiosity.

The last two centuries of the Roman period saw the introduction of small, heated structures (*colour plate 12*), usually on villa sites, which are often referred to as corn-dryers. There were two at the Halstock Villa. A T-shaped flue was fired at one end. It is not certain what lay above the heated surface, but it is certainly possible that it was for drying grain in wet seasons. However, experimental dryers have been built, particularly at the Butser Ancient Farm in Hampshire, and one of the conclusions was that the dryers were better suited to malting barley for beer making; it may be that we are seeing a revival of the native drink in the closing years of Roman Britain.

It is often said that life in the countryside changed little from Iron Age times. But this cannot be true within the boundaries of the Roman province. No doubt the Durotrigian farmer grumbled, but he lived in peace most of the time, had a larger family, fed them well, sold his produce profitably in the markets and bought himself some of the trappings of Roman civilisation in the form of clothes and ornaments. His house became rectangular, perhaps roofed in tile, distinctly drier and more comfortable. He learnt (especially if he was close to one of the more Romanised villa estates) to dry his corn in kilns and keep it in granaries – no longer was it necessary to bury the corn in the ground to preserve it.

Some suggestion has been made that the villa estates, especially in the south-west, changed the ancient landscape of Celtic fields and made their profits from large-scale sheep farming. Certainly at the Dewlish Villa small fields next to the house appear to have been obliterated and open parkland created. But at other villas where environmental evidence shows what farming operations were going on, it is clear that most of the activities of traditional mixed farming were undertaken.

7

THE VILLAS

The main sign of Romanisation in the Dorset countryside was the appearance of villas. There is not much evidence for them in the first and second centuries AD, but in the third and fourth they began to be built in greater numbers, and towards the end of Roman rule in Britain some were both large and luxurious.

The Latin word *villa* means farm and implies that it is a substantial establishment with a farmhouse built to a considerable degree of luxury. Some of the villas near Rome itself were little short of palaces. While in smaller ones the farmyard was right in front of the house, in the larger villas farming activities were carried out away from the main house, and the courtyard became a formal garden.

Some of the largest villas in Britain were very impressive indeed, and of those that can be visited perhaps Chedworth in Gloucestershire provides the best glimpse of what life for the rich was like in the Romano-British countryside. Fishbourne is even more spectacular, though it is really in a different class, being clearly a royal palace. In Dorset, many of them represented the country homes of the native Durotrigian nobility, who would also have had a luxury house in town. The wealth needed to build them came from farming, from ownership of land, and from whatever industries the nobility had their money invested in.

The increased wealth shown by the villas in the fourth century would seem to imply that the Durotriges, or at least their leaders, had become very prosperous by then. It is a little difficult to see where this prosperity came from, and because of this some historians have suggested that the explanation lies in the arrival of wealthy landowners from Gaul. Britain, particularly the west, may have seemed a haven from political troubles and Saxon attacks at this time, and rich nobles of the tribes in Gaul may have bought up modest Durotrigian villas with their land and modernised them. This is certainly a possible explanation, but at present there is not enough evidence to be certain.

The villas in Durotrigian territory are in two main groups: those around Ilchester (at least 35 are known, mostly in Somerset now) and about 15 around Dorchester. It is unusual to find large villas more than an hour or so on horseback from a town, but there were a few in the north-east of the county such as Tarrant Hinton. These may have had special functions, such as the home of a procurator in charge of an imperial estate.

49 Part of the Frampton Villa mosaic, showing the chi-rho symbol. *After Lysons*

An interesting discussion about whether villas had distinctive economies of their own, or were little different from neighbouring non-villa settlements, appears in Branigan & Miles 1988. Comparatively little research has been done on villa groupings and the economic connections between them and the towns. Nevertheless, in spite of differences in each villa history, it seems likely that they were inextricably linked with farms, villages and towns, and that the copious coinage that is found on most Roman sites represents cash-based trading.

Recognising the interrelationships between activities on villa estates forms an ongoing and significant development in the study of the Roman-British countryside, but it is waiting to be explored in connection with the Dorset evidence.

Richard Reece points out that lists of coins from villa sites need to be interpreted warily. The relationship of coins found to coins lost, coins lost to coins in circulation, or coins in circulation to coins minted, is very complicated. Reece's advice is that looking at an isolated coin list and trying to turn it into hard history is pointless. It is merely that certain characteristics can be identified, such as the financial difficulties of villa owners, whoever they were, at the end of the Roman period.

The villas of Dorset have suffered much damage over the centuries. Most were abandoned by their owners around AD 400 when growing economic and political chaos made it impossible to maintain them. Danger of attack (a possibility in Dorset, though a near certainty in many eastern parts of the province) persuaded owners to live in town and probably to transport their harvest there as soon as possible. Dorchester and Ilchester at least had walls to defend them.

The villas then suffered what every abandoned house suffers, ranging from small boys with catapults breaking the windows, to large-scale digging in medieval times to find dressed stone to use in a new church. Often little but the mosaic floors survives; the floors are useless for building material, unless of course they lie over a hypocaust or under-floor heating system. In such cases they may well have been torn up to get at the large slabs which carried them over the heating channels.

In the end the villas became slight bumps in the ground. Nevertheless, the discovery of a mosaic floor belonging to a ruined villa still provides one of the most exciting moments in archaeology as the pictures and patterns of a bygone age are uncovered. If you are fortunate enough to make such a discovery by accident, please get expert help from your local museum rather than attempt to uncover it yourself. The remains are normally very fragile indeed.

Another hazard for villas has been inexpert excavation by eighteenth- and nineteenth-century antiquarians, which has left us details of mosaic floors and little else. The mosaics are a tiny, though fascinating, part of the story. Nowadays equal attention is paid to the farm buildings and the evidence for farming, in order to build up a portrait of the people and how they lived and worked.

In fact a newly discovered villa site, which has not been 'excavated' in recent centuries is a valuable find indeed, and there is a strong case for the purchase and preservation of the site under permanent grassland, so that at some future date more advanced archaeological techniques can be brought to bear. In these circumstances the site would need protection, not only from the plough, but also from a few irresponsible treasure hunters who, in spite of the Ancient Monuments and Archaeological Areas Act of 1979, which makes it an offence, continue to damage scheduled sites in Britain.

FRAMPTON

In the water meadows beside the Frome at Frampton lies one of the first villas to be discovered in Dorset. Found in 1796, its mosaic floors were cleared and drawn by Lysons (see 49). Its main interest lies in the Christian symbol, found in the pattern of one of its mosaic floors. Although usually called the Frampton Villa, it actually lies in Maiden Newton parish. The story of its discovery and excavation is an extraordinary one.

In 1794 labourers were digging in Nunnery Meadow in the Frome Valley just below the present farm at Throop. They were said to be digging for flints. As they would not

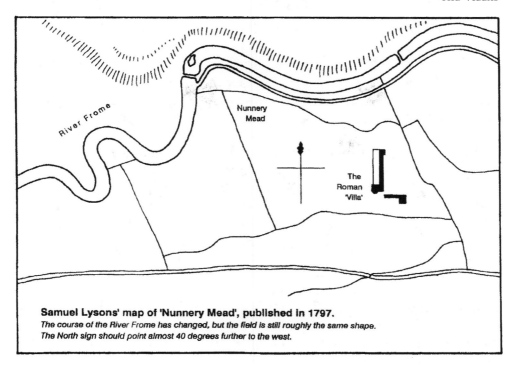

Samuel Lysons' map of 'Nunnery Mead', published in 1797.
The course of the River Frome has changed, but the field is still roughly the same shape.
The North sign should point almost 40 degrees further to the west.

50 Lysons' map of Nunnery Mead showing the overall plan of the villa (redrawn)

normally expect to find flints in the flood plain of the Frome, they probably knew about the Roman site, or at least that there was a low mound which contained lots of flints and other useful building material.

They found and uncovered the first of the mosaic floors. This was drawn by Mr James Engleheart for Mr Francis Browne, who owned Frampton Court at that time. The picture was shown at the Society of Antiquaries of London on 12 February 1795. The pavement measured about 20 x 13ft. It contained elaborate pictures possibly based on the *Metamorphoses* by the Roman poet Ovid. The drawing was seen by Samuel Lysons, the well-known antiquarian, who came to Dorset to see for himself in 1796.

By then the pavement was damaged – it had presumably been left out in the frost, or perhaps the labourers had removed flints from its foundations. Lysons noticed that there was another large mound nearly 200ft long stretching at a right angle to the original pavement, which might well cover further Roman remains.

King George III was at Weymouth with the royal family at the time. Lysons persuaded him to allow soldiers from the Royal Lancashire Regiment of Fencibles to help excavate. They were marched up from Weymouth, and camped on the site. The excavation uncovered a large double mosaic room joined by an arch, measuring about 30 x 20ft. There was also a corridor leading from there towards the north-east.

A great stir was caused by this floor, and the King and Queen came to visit on 9 September accompanied by the Princesses Augusta, Elizabeth and Mary. The floor pattern included the chi-rho emblem used in Late Roman times as a Christian symbol. It shows the Greek letters for CHR, the first three letters of Christ's name. It is possible that this room was used for Christian worship, and there is other evidence from Dorset (particularly at Hinton St Mary) that Roman villas were used as religious centres. On the other hand it may merely mean that Christianity was regarded as just another religion included along with Neptune and other gods.

The completion of the excavation was blocked by a large hayrick, and Lysons returned the following year to find yet another smaller mosaic room at the end of the 90ft-long corridor. This time he used the South Gloucestershire Regiment of Militia. The Royal Family again visited. Eleven years later Lysons published his map and drawings of the site (Lysons 1817).

The whole place is quite extraordinary. Although it is usually called the Frampton Villa, this can hardly be the case. A Roman villa was basically a farm which included a luxurious dwelling house. This site on the flood plain of the Frome, which must have been regularly flooded, would be a crazy place for a farm, and there is no evidence of domestic features. It seems to consist of three temples, joined by long corridors (50). According to Lysons there were no other buildings — presumably he searched for them, though he might not have recognised timber buildings. Was it in the flood plain because they were water gods? Did one of the temples later become used for Christian worship?

One interesting detail is that some individual pictures in the mosaics appear to have been hacked out, perhaps by Christian zealots who are known to have attacked pagan temples in the fourth century.

If it really was a religious centre such as the famous site at Lydney in Gloucestershire, then there would also be offices and probably baths and a hotel for visitors. But these might well be on more solid ground not far away, and have not so far been found. It has been suggested that the Dorchester Roman Aqueduct started here and these gods were worshipped in association with it. But it is now known that the aqueduct started at Littlewood farm, Frampton (see chapter 4), and the spring a little upstream of the 'villa' is much too low to feed the aqueduct anyway.

At the present time the site lies among the water meadows constructed in the eighteenth or nineteenth century, though now derelict. The construction of these complex channels was probably later than the excavation, and they approach the mounds of the backfilled excavation very close indeed. They would have done serious damage to any other structures nearby. It is not clear to what extent the mosaic floors survive underground at the present time.

HINTON ST MARY

Hinton St Mary is the most famous of the Dorset villas. It was discovered by accident in 1963 when the village blacksmith was digging a hole for his wife's washing line. Oddly enough the villa suffered a rather similar fate to Frampton in that we now know little more about it than can be deduced from the mosaic. This time the reason was

51 Head of Christ from the mosaic at Hinton St Mary

the enormous publicity which followed the discovery, making further archaeological research difficult.

The publicity came from the fact that the mosaic floor had at its centre a picture of the head and shoulders of Christ, backed by the chi-rho symbol (51). This is discussed in chapter 9. The floor was bought by the British Museum, and used to form a major exhibit in its Romano-British display. At the time of writing it is regrettably in store. Also on display is the complete iron grille from one of the villa's windows. There is nothing to see at the site today.

TARRANT HINTON

A large villa at Tarrant Hinton was under excavation from 1968-84, by the Wimborne Archaeological Group, and full publication has now taken place (Graham 2006) (52). The site is particularly important for the story it tells of development from the preceding Iron Age. Spectacular mosaics have not survived here and the villa lies in close proximity to a considerable area of Romano-British settlement.

The most interesting finds have been a twin-cylinder pump from its well and an inscription on a sandstone block, also thrown into the well. Both can be seen in the

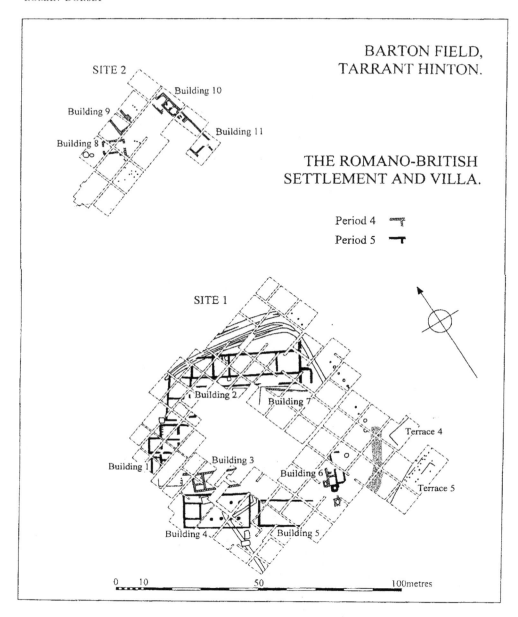

SITE 2

Building 10

Building 9

Building 11

Building 8

BARTON FIELD,
TARRANT HINTON.

THE ROMANO-BRITISH
SETTLEMENT AND VILLA.

Period 4

Period 5

SITE 1

Building 2

Building 7

Terrace 4

Building 1

Building 3

Building 6

Terrace 5

Building 4

Building 5

0   10   50   100metres

52 Plan of the Tarrant Hinton Villa. © *Dorset Natural History and Archaeological Society*

museum at the Priest's House, Wimborne. The inscription is important, as inscriptions from villas are very rare indeed. It is a tombstone from the cemetery belonging to the villa or the settlement. It reads:

CUP VEP DECESSIT ANNO XXXVIIII TUSCO
ET BASSO COS VII KAL SEPTEMB

'Cupitius Vep ... died in his 39th year in the consulship of
Tuscus and Bassus, on the 26 August'.

Mentioning the names of the consuls is a common method of naming the year, in this
case AD 258. Although the inscription mentions September, the date is actually in August,
because Roman dates are given as so many days before certain fixed points in the month
(in this case seven days, counting inclusively, before 1 September).

Cup is almost certainly short for the name Cupitius, the dead man's family name. It
occurs quite frequently, mostly in the Celtic areas of the Empire. The second name, or
cognomen, is more difficult. It appears to begin with Vep ..., but it is just possible that it
is Ver .... If it is Ver ... then it might stand for the Latin cognomen Verecundus or there
are several other possibilities. If it were Vep ... then it might be short for an unknown
Celtic name, and thus be the only Romano-British Durotrigian native to whom we can
put a name, or at least part of one! But that may be wishful thinking.

The pump is also of great interest. Made of a wooden block, with bronze and lead
working parts, it may have been worked by slaves or a treadmill to pump water from
the well. Such items of engineering were common enough in the Roman world, but
their survival is rare.

The Tarrant Hinton Villa site had a long and complex history. All the excavated
areas of the site showed evidence of occupation during the Iron Age, with a pottery
date range from the sixth century BC to the mid-first century AD. Concentrations of
pits were found adjacent to roundhouse sites and aerial photography indicates that the
excavation sampled only a small part of the settlement, the overall plan of which was
never defined.

The extent to which the settlement was continuous is unknown but by the Late
Iron Age it was clearly extensive, displaying all the features characteristic of the larger
Durotrigian Iron Age settlements of Cranborne Chase of which a number are known
from excavation. The south side of the settlement appears to have been defined by a
substantial and potentially long-lived ditch, running down the shoulder of the hill, to the
south of which two Middle Iron Age burials were found and one of the first century AD.

The large courtyard building upon which the excavations focused represents only the
final stage of the development of the site which does not appear to have taken that form
until the late third or even fourth century AD. Evidence of the nature of the settlement
in the preceding 200 years is difficult to define, though pottery and coins from both
excavated areas suggest continuous occupation from about the mid-second century AD
and probably earlier.

Some of this material came from ditches and pits which can clearly be assigned to
this earlier settlement period, and those buildings on Site 1 which do not clearly form
apart of the courtyard villa may be contemporary with these features as well as the group
of buildings excavated on Site 2. The presence of postholes on both sites and shallow
terraces indicates also the likely presence of contemporary timber structures.

The evidence for Period 4 shows a scatter of buildings across the site, the full extent
of which is unknown. Those on Site 1 possibly lie within their own enclosure, forming

a group of structures that eventually became the courtyard villa. Those on Site 2 may be only a small part of a much wider group of small buildings. That this phase of Romanised settlement developed, perhaps in a very piecemeal fashion, from an existing native Iron Age settlement seems likely and some spatial correspondence in ditches and structures can be seen. Period 4 may essentially, therefore, be a continuation of the Iron Age settlement being a small village or cluster of farms rather than a single, villa-type establishment.

In the later period of Romano-British occupation of the site the emergence of a fairly standard form of courtyard villa can be seen. Ranged around three sides of a courtyard opening to the east, the main residence was Building 1 and the west end of Building 2, forming the west range and north-west angle of the complex. The northern range comprised a number of large, rooms probably work rooms, forming the east end of Building 2, fronted by a long corridor. The south range comprised buildings 4 and 5, each being working buildings or barns rather then residential. The final phase of the small bath house, Building 6, now at the south-east angle of the courtyard, may be contemporary with this period.

Though denuded, the remains were sufficient to show a high degree of comfort and sophistication in the residential quarters, though a functional difference between Buildings 1 and 2 seems possible. Building 1 may have been the family residence, with the west end of Building 2, comprising three large and well-appointed rooms (Room 2.1 contained very finely-wrought figurative wall-paintings) used for formal functions and entertaining.

The courtyard villa in this final form did not emerge until the mid-fourth century and its development may have been piecemeal over a long period of time. It could, however, be seen as developing from the structures in Period 4, being the logical final form of a long established unit. Alternatively, it could represent a profound change in the nature of the hillside settlement, now dominated or obliterated by the villa, which was clearly a centre of great wealth and therefore power.

HALSTOCK

At Halstock a very large courtyard villa (of the group attached to Ilchester) was excavated by a series of excavators from 1967-85 (53). The excavations, in difficult conditions on a wet clay soil, have produced spectacular baths, and some of the barns and other farm buildings. The main courtyard house has sadly been ploughed well below the level of its floors so that knowledge of large parts of the villa is confined to the ground plan given by the foundations.

The site lies in the base of a broad valley on the north side of the North Dorset Downs, facing north and west into Somerset. The earliest features identified belonged to a Durotrigian settlement dateable to the mid-first century BC to mid-first century AD. This appears to have been deserted at, or just before, the Roman conquest of AD 43 and there was no evidence of subsequent occupation of the site until the construction of

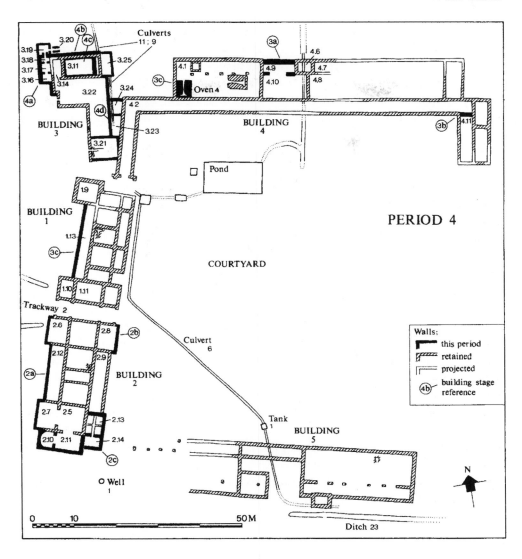

53 Plan of the Halstock Villa. © *Dorset Natural History and Archaeological Society*

the earliest villa buildings around the middle of the second century AD. The occupation of the villa appeared continuous from that date until at least the end of the fourth century. There is little certain evidence, however, for the date of its eventual decline and demise.

The villa was established on the site during the middle of the second century AD and lay 3 miles west of the Roman road between Ilchester (*Lindinis*) and Dorchester (*Durnovaria*). Four periods of development were seen beginning (Period 1) with a corridor-type building with a detached bath house to the north-west, in loose association with two, large hall-like buildings, one within a separate enclosure to the south-east.

In this stage, as subsequently, the focal and specifically residential building around which the west range developed, can be distinguished from the working structures of the villa which were ultimately incorporated into a north and south range.

The third century saw large-scale changes (Periods 2 and 3), culminating in a courtyard-type villa of three linked ranges; a west range comprising the main residence or residences, Building 1 and Building 2; a north range comprising large, single-aisled hall fronted by a long portico, Building 4; and a comparable south range, Building 5, which incorporated at least one single-aisled hall. An extensive bath house, Building 3, lay slightly detached to the north-west (*colour plate 11*). From Period 2 there was evidence of a system of water supply originating from a spring in the southern part of the site, which by Period 3 was rebuilt to supply a probably ornamental pond and tanks in the north-west part of the courtyard.

The changes of Period 3 which resulted in the creation of a courtyard villa with evident architectural unity can be dated to the late third century, which is the only well-established chronological point in the villa's development. Subsequent changes belong to the fourth century and were embellishments of the existing courtyard structure rather than expansion. Extensive change was, however, made to the bath house, perhaps reflecting changes in social practices, and two mosaics were laid in the large rooms of the altered structure. These date to the first half of the fourth century and belonged to the Corinian school of mosaicists (from Cirencester). Changes made to Building 2 appeared to reflect its increased importance and perhaps dominance as the focal dwelling of the west range.

In large part due to the denuded state of the remains, the functions of specific buildings of the villa settlement are difficult to define except in general terms such as residence, bath house and work-hall. The large areas in Room 4.1 of the north range could have been used for grain drying on a large scale (*colour plate 12*) and there is evidence for roasting germinated grain, perhaps indicating the production of a wheat-based ale. Debris from iron smithing was found in several areas, with a concentration, however, on the east end of Building 4.

Other activities for which there was limited evidence in the south range were bone working and bronze working. Objects reflecting the probable agricultural base of the villa economy were, however, scarce, being limited to an iron reaping hook and an ox goad. The collection of animal bone from the excavations showed the wide range of domestic animals present. Though there was a preponderance of older animals, many young animals may have been driven live to markets elsewhere.

Significant villa sites which may be regarded as attached to *Lindinis* (Ilchester), and approximate location:

Bratton Seymour	ST 66 29
Broadwell	ST 40 24
Catsgore	ST 50 25
Charlton Mackrell, Bull Lawn Lane	ST 51 29

Charlton Mackrell, Windmill Hill Wood	ST 51 29
Chedzoy	ST 44 37
Dinnington	ST 40 13
Ditcheat	ST 64 34
East Coker	ST 54 13
Ham Hill	ST 49 16
High Ham	ST 42 29
Huish Episcopi	ST 42 27
Hurcot	ST 51 29
Ilchester Mead	ST 51 22
Kingsdon	ST 52 27
Littleton	ST 49 31
Lopen	ST 42 14
Low Ham	ST 43 28
Lufton	ST 51 17
Lytes Cary	ST 53 29
Melbury	ST 47 27
Montacute	ST 48 16
Norton sub Hamdon	ST 46 15
Pitney I	ST 45 30
Pitney II	ST 44 29
Seavington St Mary	ST 40 13
Somerton	ST 49 29
Somerton, Barcombe Hill	ST 49 29
Somerton, Bradley Hill	ST 48 30
Somerton, Etsome Farm	ST 48 31
South Petherton, Jailers Mill	ST 44 17
South Petherton, Watergore	ST 43 15
Street	ST 48 34
West Coker, Chessels	ST 52 13
Yeovil, Westlands	ST 54 15

Significant villa sites which may be regarded as attached to *Durnovaria* (Dorchester), and approximate location:

Askerswell	SY 52 93
Charminster	SY 66 94
Corscombe	SY 53 05
Dewlish	SY 76 97
Dorchester, Olga Road	SY 68 90
Frampton	SY 61 95
Grimstone	SY 63 95

Owermoigne	SY 77 85
Piddletrenthide	SY 72 00
Preston	SY 70 82
Rampisham	SY 56 04
Weymouth	SY 67 78
Wynford Eagle	SY 57 95

Significant villa sites which do not lie close to *Lindinis* or *Durnovaria*:

Bradford Abbas I	ST 59 15
Bradford Abbas II	ST 57 15
Brenscombe	SY 97 82
Bucknowle	SY 95 81
Castleton	ST 65 17
Charlton Marshall	ST 90 03
Church Knowle	SY 93 82
Fifehead Neville	ST 77 11
Halstock	ST 53 07
Hinton Parva	SU 00 03
Hinton St Mary	ST 78 16
Iwerne Minster	ST 85 13
Minchington	ST 97 14
Pamphill	ST 97 04
Sherborne	ST 62 15
Shillingstone	ST 82 11
Tarrant Hinton	ST 92 11
Thornford	ST 51 39
Witchampton, Abbey Mead	ST 99 06
Witchampton, Hemsworth	ST 96 05

For details of other possible sites with slight or doubtful evidence, and for main references, see Scott 1993.

1 Aerial photograph of Dorchester showing Maumbury Rings and the possible site of the Roman fort (left of centre). © *Francesca Radcliffe*

2 Excavation of the baths of Roman Dorchester in 1977

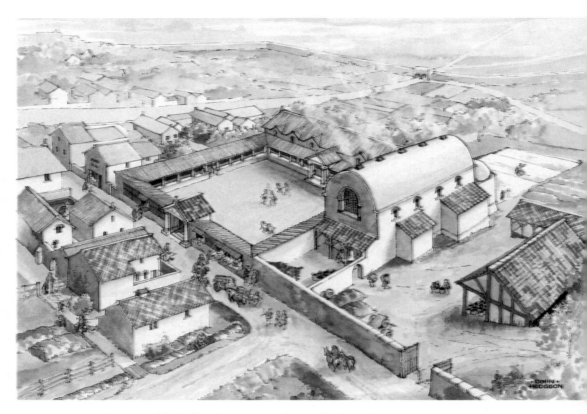

3 Reconstruction drawing of the baths of Roman Dorchester. © *John Hodgson*

Opposite above: 4 Aerial photograph of the Roman signal station on Black Down

Opposite below: 5 Building the Dorchester aqueduct. © *John Hodgson*

6 Aerial photograph showing the Roman army labour camp at Littlewood Farm, Frampton (centre). © *Francesca Radcliffe*

Opposite above: 7 The *castellum divisiorum* of the Roman aqueduct in Dorchester. © *John Hodgson*

Opposite below: 8 Excavation of aqueduct 1B at Frampton, showing its complex structure

9 Painted plaster from a Roman Christian mausoleum at Poundbury, showing praying figure

Opposite above: 10 Reconstruction drawing of the Roman Town House in Dorchester. © *John Hodgson*

Opposite below: 11 The swimming pool in the baths at the Halstock Roman Villa

12 A corn-drying kiln (or barley-malter) at Halstock Roman Villa

Opposite above: 13 Dewlish Roman Villa – Room 6, the entrance hall of the villa

Opposite below: 14 Dewlish Roman Villa – Room 4, showing surviving wall plaster *in situ*

15 Dewlish Roman Villa – Room 9, showing damaged hypocaust

Opposite above: *16* Dewlish Roman Villa – general view of Room 11 and the veranda

Opposite below: *17* Dewlish Roman Villa – the leopard mosaic fragment in Room 11

18 Dewlish Roman Villa – the mosaic of the dining apse

Opposite above: 19 Dewlish Roman Villa – fragment of inscription of wall plaster

Opposite below: 20 Dewlish Roman Villa – later mosaic in Room 25 (the baths' changing room)

21 Dewlish Roman Villa – earlier mosaic in Room 25 (the baths' changing room)

22 Dewlish Roman Villa – the cold plunge bath in Room 26

23 Reconstruction drawing of the Dewlish Roman Villa. © *John Hodgson*

24 Excavation of the Roman road in Thorncombe Wood, near Dorchester

25 Antefixes (roof ornaments) from excavations in Dorchester. © *Wessex Archaeology*

THE DEWLISH ROMAN VILLA

For 11 years from 1968-79 the villa at Dewlish (near Puddletown) was the training excavation of the Dorset Institute of Higher Education (formerly the Weymouth College of Education).

The site in the grounds of Dewlish House has a complex history (54). The dry summer of 1976 revealed many features in parchmarks in the grass. The earliest occupation was a very wide scatter of Mesolithic flints dating to about 6000 BC. There is also a farm of Iron Age date (not excavated) with its many grain storage pits and field enclosures. This was followed by small square 'Celtic' fields of the early part of the Roman period, but no trace of the farm of this date was found, and it is impossible to say whether it was a villa.

In the late third century AD a small farm was built, just about qualifying as a villa. A single long building housed the owner at one end and the barn at the other. There were no mosaics, but the walls were plastered and painted. Early in the fourth century these early buildings were converted entirely into enlarged farm buildings, and a larger luxury house was built on a second side of the courtyard, with a full length veranda and central porch. But still the floors were wooden or rammed earth.

After a short life the villa was abandoned and allowed to fall down in part. Whether the same fate befell the farm is not clear, but it is unlikely. Then in the second half of the fourth century either prosperity returned or, more likely, the property was bought for renovation. The house was rebuilt, in some parts from the foundations up. The farm buildings were cleared away entirely, and in their place appeared a small temple and priest's house. The small fields were abandoned and the surrounding area became parkland. The villa had become a small pagan religious settlement.

The baths were enlarged – perhaps healing was a central feature of the cult – and almost every room in the main building was fitted with mosaic floors. At the back a huge kitchen block was built, presumably to cope with the visitors. The plan of the building at this stage in its history is shown in *Figure 55*. There are some 51 rooms, all on the ground floor. It is clear that the villa is a bungalow, as in the main house (Rooms 1-30) much of which is well preserved, there are no narrow spaces which could have been stairs.

It is difficult to interpret the uses of rooms in a villa, but in certain areas the structural evidence makes this possible. Room 4 with its three-sided apse, is heated by a channelled

54 Rediscovery of the Dewlish Roman Villa

hypocaust with its stokehole outside the apse. Like every room in this building at this stage of its history it has a mosaic floor. It was clearly used as a living room by the owners when they were in residence in the winter months. Rooms 1, 2 and 3 were probably bedrooms. They are small, and the mosaic in Room 3 is of particular interest. A narrow strip of decoration runs down the long axis of the room. The sides are of very coarse *tesserae* (the small pieces that make up a mosaic) and are not intended to be seen. It is likely that the sides were covered by beds. This north-east wing of the building is reasonably secluded from the activity of the other areas.

The mosaic in Room 4 had been mostly destroyed by the retrieval of the stone slabs carrying the floor over the heating channels, probably in the later Middle Ages. However, the apse was one of the few areas of the villa where stone retrieval had not occurred, making it possible to see the pattern of the final collapse of the building (*colour plate 14*).

The floor itself had been clear of furniture or other debris at the time of collapse. Directly on the floor lay fragments of the window glass. These were covered by fragments of painted plaster from the walls, brought down by the frost and rain as the roof deteriorated. On top of this were several stone tiles from the roof, giving a useful indication of the roof structure at this point. Finally flints and mortar from the upper part of the walls completed the layers. It was clear throughout the villa that the walls were flint and mortar up to full height. The sheer volume of flints ruled out any possibility of half-timbered construction.

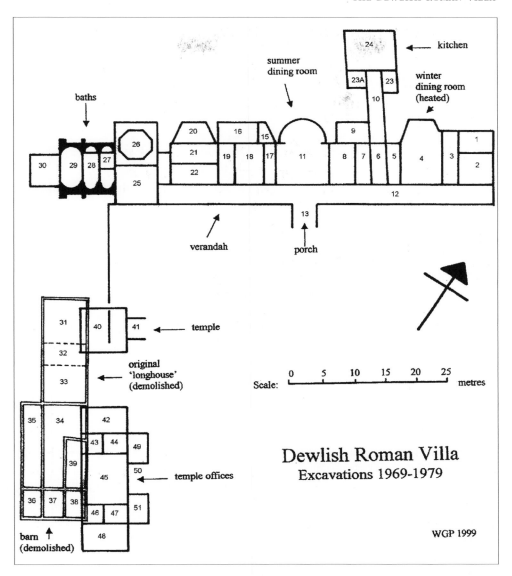

baths

summer
dining room

24 ← kitchen

winter
dining room
(heated)

verandah

porch

temple

original
'longhouse'
(demolished)

Scale:

0   5   10   15   20   25
                              metres

Dewlish Roman Villa
Excavations 1969-1979

temple offices

barn
(demolished)

WGP 1999

55 Plan of the Dewlish Roman Villa

Room 6 with its Greek key-pattern mosaic (*colour plate 13*) was the only room between Rooms 1 and 8 that had a door onto the veranda. The internal walls all had traces of their interconnecting doors into the other rooms. Room 6 (slightly out of true in its layout) led through another door into passage 10, which led to the kitchen (Room 24) and probable storerooms (23 and 23A). Wooden floors were used throughout this working area. This was proved by the presence of wall plaster *in situ*, showing a straight bottom edge where it terminated at the floorboards. Room 24 had been severely damaged by ploughing, but traces of the ovens survived.

Rooms 5 and 7 were anterooms, providing preparation space for the serving of meals in either Room 4 or Room 11 (see below). Room 8 had been the kitchen in the previous stage of the villa's history, and an oven base was found beneath the coarse mosaic floor. Room 9 had a simple mosaic floor and its own channelled hypocaust, and opened onto the kitchen passage. It is tempting to see it as the office of the housekeeper. Interestingly two sections of its hypocaust channel still carried the covering slabs, making it possible to crawl below the Roman floor (*colour plate 15*).

Room 11 was undoubtedly the focus of entertainment in the villa. It had no hypocaust, and so was unlikely to be used in the winter. But it is the largest room, it is centrally placed, and it is directly opposite the porch giving access onto the veranda. The partition between Room 11 and the veranda was at least for a time a slot rather than a wall, suggesting that sliding doors may have been opened onto the garden on summer evenings.

Room 11 had a spectacular and expensive mosaic (*colour plate 16*). The villa was originally discovered when a tree blew over in 1740, uncovering a mosaic. Alas, this appears to have happened right in the middle of Room 11, destroying much of the floor. Nevertheless the south-east corner of the main room survives, showing a leopard killing a gazelle. The quality is very fine indeed (*colour plate 17*). This fragment of mosaic was lifted during the excavation and can be seen when Dewlish House is open to the public. The semi-circular apse also survived mainly intact. This mosaic (*colour plate 18*) remains in the ground. (For a full description of this and other mosaics in the villa, see below.)

A considerable quantity of painted wall plaster was found, from this and other rooms. However, attempts at reconstruction of patterns have not been very successful, owing to the moving of the plaster and further damage to it during stone retrieval at various times. Much of the fallen plaster in Room 11 appears to have been shovelled onto the veranda, mixed with that from other rooms, and shovelled back again.

Rooms 11 and 8 play an important part in dating the final phase of the villa's history. The wall between Room 11 and Room 8 was rebuilt from its foundations at this time, and the new mosaics laid on either side. Coins trapped beneath the floor in Room 8 gave a latest date of AD 356, and the rebuilding must have happened at or after this date.

The function of Rooms 15-19 is less certain. All this group had mosaics, and 16 had a channelled hypocaust. They may have been a suite of rooms for visitors. Rooms 20-22 however provide an unsolved puzzle. Room 20 had a hypocaust, but 21 and 22 were initially water tanks lined with *opus signinum*, but later filled with rubble and presumably floored over, though ploughing had removed the top levels. Perhaps the water tanks were reservoirs for the baths prior to a later running water supply, but it would be unusual to include these in the main structure of the house.

At the end of the veranda was the doorway leading into the baths. The functions of the rooms is clear. Room 25 was the *apodyterium* or changing room, 26 the *frigidarium* or cold plunge, 27 an anteroom, 28 the *tepidarium* or warm room, 29 the *caldarium* or hot room, and 30 the *praefurnium* or stokehole and fuel store.

Room 25 was the only room in the whole building where one mosaic was replaced by another. A substantial part of both survived, and both can be seen in Dorset County

56 Marks made by the hobnailed footwear of a workman building the baths of the Dewlish Roman Villa

Museum. The contrast in fashion is spectacular. The earlier floor is entirely geometric in pattern (*colour plate 21*), while the later is a splendid frieze of fabulous sea–creatures (*colour plate 20*) swimming round a central picture, possibly of the god Neptune. The procession is led by Cupid riding a dolphin. For further discussion of these mosaics see below.

Room 26 (*colour plate 22*) has a cold–water tank floored with white *tesserae* and boasting a surrounding seat covered in slabs of Kimmeridge shale (see *73*). It must have been a splendid sight when first completed. A niche in each corner of the room probably contained a statue.

Rooms 27-29 had been severely damaged by the retrieval of useful stone from its pillared hypocausts, and very little remained except the sub–floor and the bases of a few pillars. In Room 28 there was a glimpse into the process of construction of the baths. After the laying of the sub–floor concrete a workman in size 9 hobnailed footwear had walked on wet concrete and his footprints remain to this day (*56*).

Room 30 was built over the site of a deep pit, which caused much discussion as to its purpose. It measured 2 x 3 x 5m deep. It was full of building rubble, though this cannot have been the purpose for which it was dug. The likeliest explanation is that it was a cold store, a common feature of Roman sites, though not always recognised. A second one lay at a different date at the north-west end of Room 31.

Rooms 31-39 formed the earliest building on the villa site. Unfortunately at this end of the excavation ploughing had removed all the floors, leaving only the lowest courses of the foundations. Rooms 31-33 had stone exterior walls, but wooden partitions with painted-plaster surfaces. It is likely that this was a simple farmhouse of 'long house'

Left: 57 Column of Portland stone used in the temple at the Dewlish Roman Villa

Below: 58 Crucible and tuyère from the Dewlish Roman Villa

style, with initially Rooms 34 and 39 forming the farming end of the building. When the main house was built in its first pre-mosaic stage, all the farm buildings were given over to agriculture, and the barn end expanded by the addition of Rooms 35–38 and presumably a total rebuilding.

When the main house received its mosaics, all the farming activity was removed from the immediate locality and Rooms 31–39 demolished. In its place came a temple, Room 40. It is difficult to see any other explanation for a single room with columns (57) and a grand porch, and a (totally destroyed) fine mosaic floor. The revival of pagan religion initiated by the emperor Julian in AD 461 may have led to the establishment of a rural religious site at Dewlish, paralleled most famously at Lydney in Gloucestershire with the temple of Nodens. We do not know the name of the god worshipped at Dewlish.

The temple was destroyed by fire of an intensity that cracked even the stones in the foundations. This may have been an accident of course, but there is the possibility that Christian zealots came to Dewlish to put a violent end to the worship of a pagan god.

Rooms 42 to 51 were clearly built at the same time as the temple, as they are in alignment with it. They may have been accommodation or offices associated with the cult. Success did not last long; by about AD 400 the building was in ruins again, though the farming no doubt continued. But the farm buildings associated with the grand phase of the villa were clearly on another site and have not been found. How far the history of Dewlish villa is typical, remains to be seen. Nothing of the villa is to be seen at Dewlish today, as the site has been filled in and re-seeded.

Surprisingly few artefacts were found during the excavation. Perhaps this should not be surprising. This was a sophisticated household during the main part of its existence. Rubbish will not have been thrown out of the back door, but deposited in bins and at intervals carted away to perhaps a disused quarry in the woods, which is unlikely to be found except by accident.

If it were not for the two abandoned cold stores we would have a very poor record indeed. After these fulfilled their function, they were used temporarily as rubbish pits, and all sorts of debris was deposited in them. This final period of their use coincided with reconstruction of the house, and the fill included many fragments of painted wall plaster, flints, roof tiles and considerable quantities of broken pottery.

Perhaps the most interesting find in the cold store later covered by Room 30 was a bronze worker's crucible and a fragment of the furnace including a tuyère, the nozzle of the bellows (58). This provides useful evidence that an estate such as this would have possessed all the craftsmen necessary for its upkeep, most of them being slaves of the owners, and including carpenters and blacksmiths.

Fragments of the house itself were found, both in the pits and incorporated into, for example, later floor foundations. The large quantity of flints has already been mentioned. These were not flaked to produce a flat surface as often done in recent centuries in English chalk villages. They were in fact not visible at all. The survival of the base of walls, particularly in the area of Rooms 5, 6 and 7, shows that the walls were rendered inside and out. The outside was probably lime-washed, and the interior painted in *fresco*.

Left: 59 Finial from the roof of Room 11 in the Dewlish Roman Villa

Below: 60 Reconstructing the wall plaster from Room 6 of the Dewlish Roman Villa

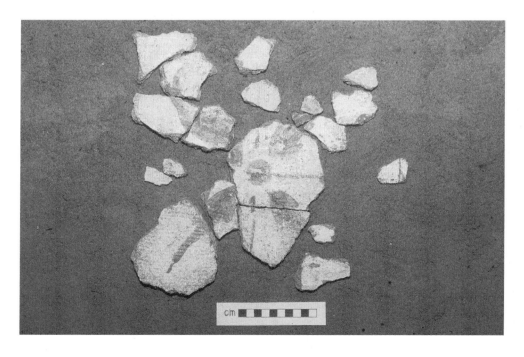

It is difficult if not impossible to construct corners of walls in flint, and many quoins were found, some *in situ*, usually of Portland stone. Details of the roof and ceilings can be convincingly reconstructed and are shown on the drawing by John Hodgson (*colour plate 23*). The main block was roofed with diamond-pattern Purbeck stone tiles, while the veranda had a clay tile roof of the familiar Roman *tegula* and *imbrex*. Most spectacular of the roofing materials was the finial (*59*) which had fallen from the apex of the roof of Room 11 and lay on the mosaic floor directly under its position on the roof. This is on display in Dorset County Museum. It is made of hamstone from the quarries on Ham Hill near Ilchester. Much of the dressed stone used in the villa came from here.

Much of the plaster (*60*) at the Dewlish Roman Villa remained more or less where it fell, until stone robbing and ploughing in recent centuries caused substantial disturbance. The effect of this was to mingle plaster from various rooms, so that it was difficult, in many cases, to determine which room a particular design might have come from. The main or north-west wing was more deeply buried and so less disturbed than the south-west wing. Due to its position on a south-west facing slope, the south-west wing was ploughed down to its foundations. Most of the plaster from the aisled barn, also from the priest's house and the shrine, was broken up by ploughing and weathering and irretrievably lost.

Stone retrieval was a major problem after the villa had fallen into ruin. Evidence of clay pipes in Room 4 indicated work in the eighteenth century, and it may well have begun much earlier. Systematic digging had cleared and destroyed the mosaic floors of rooms where hypocausts existed with their large, useful, slabs of stone bridging the channels or pillars. This involved total disturbance of the layers of rubble and plaster lying on the floors. The number of rooms with undisturbed areas of plaster was very small indeed.

Huge quantities of plaster had thus been shifted about within the villa ruin. For example, the veranda (Room 12) was found to contain plaster that probably came from inside the rooms opening on to it, along with painted plaster from the walls and ceiling of the veranda itself. It may be that, in order to reach the floors and dig them up, stone robbers would necessarily have had to shovel away the plaster first, and where better than out through the doorways onto the veranda?

However, the fragments of the wall plaster included some which also shed light on the roof and ceilings. Two fragments (*61*) which had been pressed into the upper corner of a room next to the wall plate carried the impression of all three elements, the wall, the ceiling and the rafters. The rafters were at 20° to the ceiling, confirming that the Dewlish Villa conformed to the usual pattern of low-angle Roman roofs.

In addition it was possible to detect whether plaster had fallen from a wall or a ceiling. That from the walls carried the matrix of flints or other stonework on its back, while that from the ceilings held the matrix of reed bundles (*62*), tied to the ceiling joists to carry the plaster surface. Such a construction was still being used in nineteenth-century Britain.

The reconstruction of the painted patterns on the wall plaster was a disappointment. The disturbance of the house during stone retrieval in more recent centuries made it

61 Fragments of plaster from the Dewlish Roman Villa showing the angle of the roof

difficult to obtain more than the briefest idea of the room decoration. Most intriguing was a single fragment of plaster (*colour plate 19*) carrying two letters from an inscription. The letter V or U is followed by possibly an O. A frantic search failed to produce any other part of the inscription, but it is not too fanciful to imagine a picture on the wall of a mythological scene, with a quotation from Vergil beneath it. There is little doubt that members of the household would have been able to read it.

There were two types of hypocaust, the under-floor heating system. In Rooms 4, 9 and 16 a channelled hypocaust provided gentle heating when the house was in use in winter. In the baths pillared hypocausts provided the more intense heat required for bathing. Unfortunately the small square tiles that make up the pillars are useful for lots of purposes at any period of history and very few remain.

Traces were found of the roof structure of the baths at two different periods. In its first phase hollow-tile voussoirs were used to construct the insulated roof arches, and remarkably a complete specimen survived (*63*). In the second and final phase light-weight blocks of tufa (quarried locally in Dewlish) were used. These also had a strong insulating capacity in view of the air spaces contained in the rock. Some of these were later incorporated into the foundations of Dewlish church.

The final and most interesting feature of the baths' construction for which evidence was found was the use of cavity walls. Several fragments were found of *tegulae mammatae* (*64*). Each of these square clay tiles when complete had four balls of clay attached before firing, and when placed against the main flint wall of the baths provided an effective cavity. They can be seen in use in several of the baths at Pompeii.

62 Fallen plaster showing the impression of ceiling reeds on its back from the Dewlish Roman Villa

The excavation produced a considerable quantity of pottery sherds, giving a glimpse of the purchasing pattern of the housekeeper; 20,200 sherds were found, weighing 220kg. Of these, 88 per cent were of Black Burnished Ware, manufactured in Purbeck (see chapter 10 for a description of this industry). The number of pots bought by an establishment such as Dewlish for its kitchens will have been considerable. It is interesting to speculate on whether slaves were sent to Dorchester for such purchases or, in view of the scale involved, whether sales representatives came direct from the potteries to the large villas.

For the finer wares used at table it is noticeable that samian ware was not present. This fine red pottery made mostly in Gaul and Germany was the market leader in the first and second centuries AD, but after about AD 220 it was no longer obtainable. In response Romano-British potteries stepped into the gap in the market. At Dewlish 8 per cent of the pottery found came from the potteries of the New Forest, and a little under 1 per cent from those at Oxford.

The absence of samian provides firm proof that the villa site was not in occupation till at least the second half of the third century AD. A total of 108 Roman coins were found during the villa excavation. Of these 79 were in unsealed contexts and consequently of only general interest for the history of the villa. A total of 33 coins were in sealed contexts, thus providing considerable help in dating the villa's phases. Looking purely at the chronological distribution of all the coins, a pattern can be seen. A very small scatter of coins occurs from approximately the beginning through to the middle of the third century, which is paralleled by a scatter of samian and early Black Burnished Ware from a nearby site which is at present unlocated.

63 Complete tile voussoir from the Dewlish Roman Villa

After this there is a cluster of coins from the 250s to the end of the third century, with a peak in the 280s, which represents the period of the first and second villas. This is followed by a gap until the 330s and 340s, which may suggest that the site is derelict during this time. Seen as a whole, the large number of coins from the 330s to the end of the fourth century must represent the occupation of the third villa with its temple complex. The complete cessation of coins later than 402 coincides, as was the case all over Britain, with a generally assumed end to an importation of coins minted in the Empire to the British Isles. Thus a basic three-phase sequence of coin loss may reflect phases of activity and decline on the villa site, although the coins by themselves cannot be conclusive.

It may be that coins are more likely to have been dropped and remained lost during a building or rebuilding phase than during a tranquil, habitational phase, when floors were presumably swept regularly and dropped or lost objects of any kind likely to be retrieved. Bearing in mind that few coins minted in the Empire were believed to have arrived in Britain after approximately 402, the steep increase in coins found on the site dated 388-402 may mean that coins of those dates continued in circulation for longer than normal owing to lack of replenishment, and thus afforded a longer period of opportunity for those coins to be dropped and lost. Lack of evidence of coins after 402 is not firm evidence of the end of the villa, and it may well have continued in use some way into the fifth century.

The most significant coins from the whole site were three which were all sealed beneath the coarse mosaic in Room 8, known to have been laid for the third villa. The

64 Fragment of a *tegula mammata* from the Dewlish Roman Villa

latest of these was dated 353-6 and provides an important and convincing *terminus post quem* for the third villa, as the mosaic must have been laid after 353-6. This places the third villa construction well into the second half of the fourth century and at least 80 years after the second phase of villa construction.

THE MOSAICS

The following comments on the more important mosaics are extracted and abbreviated from the report by Stephen R. Cosh in the major work on the mosaics of Roman Britain, written with David S. Neal (Cosh & Neal 2004). They will also appear in the forthcoming report on the Dewlish Villa itself (Mick & Putnam, forthcoming).

The mosaic in Room 11 was the finest and paved a large, apsed reception room opposite an elaborate porch. The mosaics in Rooms 4-17 have several features in common and give every appearance of being of a single phase (except, perhaps, the portico mosaic). The rooms are symmetrically arranged, including two similarly-shaped Rooms 9 and 16 projecting at the rear with channelled hypocausts and two rooms at either end of the range with three-sided apses.

Room 4 towards the north-eastern end has a mosaic; the floor of the more enigmatic south-western room had been ploughed out. The design of the mosaic in Room 4, with a coarse, simple-chequered pavement in the apse where couches would obscure the pavement, suggests that it was a winter *triclinium* as proposed for a similar heated room with mosaics such as those at Low Ham (Somerset), Colerne (Wiltshire) and Wigginton (Oxfordshire); these are all located at the end of the range. Rooms 1-3 may therefore represent a later addition at the south-east end of the building; and it is perhaps significant that the mosaics have no features in common with the others and, like the portico, have borders of a different colour.

Therefore, these perhaps postdate the other pavements for which coins below the mosaic in Room 8 provide a *terminus post quem* of AD 353. Alterations and enlargements were also made to the bath-suite at the south-west end. The *frigidarium/apodyterium* (Room 25), with a fine octagonal plunge bath (Room 26), was successively paved by Mosaics A and B, of which the latter has stylistic affinities with the majority of pavements in the main building. The shrine-like structure near the main house also probably had a mosaic originally.

No close parallels for the mosaics can be cited from other sites in the region; although some motifs are comparable with those on some *Durnovarian* Group pavements, there is insufficient stylistic evidence to attribute the Dewlish mosaics to that group (see below). The mosaics panels are executed in dark grey, white and red, and only on the figures are other colours introduced. The standard of workmanship is not high, again except on the figures — the leopard and antelope panel in Room 11 is among the finest drawn examples on any fourth-century pavement. Perhaps this and other lost figures were prefabricated away from the site; differences in the mortar of the bedding support this theory.

Room 4

Found 1971. Dimensions: room (including apse) 10.30 x 6m; Panel A: about 4.30m (?)square. *Tesserae*: dark grey, white and red, 15mm; border and apse: red and white, 28mm. Post AD 350. Room 4 had a channelled hypocaust separated during the excavations by a baulk from a three-sided apse to the north-west. In the main part of the room the mosaic (Panel A) had been almost completely destroyed by stone robbers, whereas Panel B in the apse was virtually untouched.

Panel A

Part of a broad border of coarse red *tesserae* survived by the south-western wall of the room, with traces of a band of simple guilloche which appears to turn at right angles some distance short of the apse. The coarse tessellation outside this continues parallel to the south-west wall, perhaps indicating that there was originally a rectangular panel between Panel A and B, but this is conjectural because the rows of red *tesserae* of the borders do not always run parallel to the panels on other floors at this site. Towards the centre, bridging a hypocaust channel, was a fragment with another band of simple guilloche parallel to the first, and two dark grey double fillets and part of a row of wave pattern of distinctive open type that also occurs in Room 17. The mosaic also has close affinities to those in Rooms 11 and 16.

Panel B

By contrast, the apse is floored in chequers of coarse red and white *tesserae* (*colour plate 14*), with a red band beside the north–west wall. It is unusual in that the tapering side walls cut obliquely across the chequer design as though built over a floor from a previous phase, but the two parts of the floor must be contemporary because below it is the channelled–hypocaust flue leading to the main part of the room. It is not known how far south the chequer design extends and the point where the apse walls met the main room was unexcavated. However, the chequers are set at a slight angle, which suggests that the plan of the room was not perfectly symmetrical. The poor–quality mosaic of the apse (as opposed to the fine wall–painting) may indicate that it was covered by furniture, such as couches, and that the room may have functioned as a *triclinium* presumably for winter use.

Room 6 (*colour plate 13*)

Found 1971, 1975. Dimensions: room 6.60 x 2m; panel 4.60 x 1m. *Tesserae*: dark grey and white, 13mm; border: red, 38mm. Post AD 350. Room 6, presumably a passage, has a long rectangular panel of bold simple meander with double returns in dark grey on a white ground within a dark grey linear frame and a white double fillet in larger *tesserae*. A border of coarse red *tesserae* surrounds it. The pattern is truncated by the border on the north–west side. This design is also used in the veranda.

Room 9 (*colour plate 15*)

Found 1971. Dimensions: room 3.10m by 4.70m. *Tesserae*: dark grey, white and red, 10mm; border: red, 32mm. Post AD 353.

The mosaic was constructed over a channelled hypocaust, which had been extensively robbed; consequently little survived, except along the north–west wall. It comprised a rectangular panel which can be reconstructed as a dark grey linear grid, probably five squares wide, with each square divided diagonally and shaded in red and white to give the effect of a chessboard pattern of triangles. The mosaic is unusual in that it is executed in finer *tesserae* than might be expected for such a simple design. It has a border of coarse red *tesserae*. Chessboard patterns of triangles occur at many sites, but normally incidental to or bordering the main scheme. Perhaps the most significant example is from Pitney, Somerset, a mosaic possibly attributable to the *Durnovarian* Group, but the colours differ and it is not imposed upon a grid as in the mosaic under discussion.

Room 11 (*colour plate 16*)

Found 1972. Dimensions: room 10.20 (max) x 7.35m. *Tesserae*: dark grey, white and red, figured work only: grey and brown, 13mm; border: red, 25mm. Post AD 353. Leopard and antelope compartment lifted and kept at Dewlish House, eastern corner fragment lifted and in Dorset County Museum, remainder reburied.

Room 11 is bipartite and divided by responds separating an apse at the north–western end; it may have been a summer *triclinium* or main reception room. It was assumed that the rectangular area (Panel A) had been largely destroyed by an uprooted tree and, therefore, was the mosaic discovered in the eighteenth century, but the description of the black–and–white mosaic scarcely matches this pavement. By contrast, the apse (Panel B) is fairly well preserved.

Panel A

Probably the rectangular area had an almost square central panel, perhaps with a circle, surrounded by alternate square and rectangular compartments, the square ones being located in the corners and midway along each side. The scheme is drawn in simple guilloche in dark grey, red and white (as is all guilloche on this mosaic). Parts of three squares survived in the corners, all with guilloche mats unusually edged in red. Only one corner of the square midway along the north-east side remained, and contains a circular red band edged in dark grey within which can be seen figurative work, perhaps the shoulder of an inward-facing bust; this would be one of four and perhaps represented Winds or Seasons. The one surviving spandrel is emphasised by a single red line.

The best preserved of the rectangular compartments, with their red linear frames, contains a fine rendering of an antelope pounced upon by a leopard (*colour plate 17*) and with blood dripping from a wound. This scene is also inward-facing, as are those in all the other surviving compartments. The two rectangular compartments on either side of the postulated bust are very fragmentary. One shows the right leg of a man who is taking up a typical spear-bearing stance; part of a spear can be seen and the top of his left brown boot survives. There is brown ground line or shadow outlined grey in front of each foot. He stands before a tree of which the lower trunk and basal leaf remain; in front of him is part of a bush or possibly part of a trailing cloak.

The pose is similar to a panel on a mosaic from nearby Frampton identified as Cadmus slaying a serpent, but a mythological interpretation here does not fit well with the hunting theme of the antelope and leopard panel. However, a hunter taking up a similar stance and confronting a leopard appears on the large apsed mosaic from Frampton, but at Dewlish there seems insufficient space to show the quarry. The other rectangular compartment has what appears to be a trunk and basal leaf of a tree in the centre. The tips of two possible hooves can be detected to the left of the tree with a ground line or shadow of brown outlined grey similar to that beneath the antelope. Burning on this compartment makes the interpretation of some parts and the isolated fragments difficult. Deer with trees in the background are typical of this area, notably on *Durnovarian* Group mosaics, and this may be another example, but more likely it is a boar as the legs appear to be short. The animal is perhaps meant to be viewed in conjunction with the hunter panel (but separated by the medallion in the axial compartment).

Only the eastern corner of the central panel survived. The linear frame is this time dark grey with an additional two rows of grey on the north-east side. Such adjustment would seem unnecessary in a rectangular compartment and may indicate a spandrel created by a central circle, and the axis of the figure or motif at 45° seems to support this view. Three slightly curved spikes point to the corner, flanked by thick, tapering curved elements, one slightly invading the frame – perhaps more evidence of difficulties caused by poor geometry. It has been argued that this represents the wing, neck and body of a gryphon. In this case the three-spiked feature would represent a wing; but such an inept depiction is hardly in accordance with the remarkably realistic portrayal of the leopard and its prey in the adjacent panel. If this were a spandrel, then the gryphon would be upside-down for it is normal for figures and motifs to face into the corners of the room (except occasionally where they lie very close to the corners).

More likely it represents the lower portion of one of four bicaudal tritons or anguipede giants supporting a circle as on a pavement from Horkstow, Lincs; the serpentine legs would have coiled into the angles of the spandrels and the arms would be upraised to support a central medallion. In this respect it would resemble a fourth-century mosaic from Trier, which also has trees and running animals at the margin, although the workmanship is quite different.

Panel B (colour plate 18)

Between the responds, and separating the large square panel from the apse, is a narrow rectangular panel of which only the north-east end survived. It comprises a scroll with red leaves with central red and white circles, emanating from sheaths. This was presumably repeated along its entire length originally, although it is possible that it sprang from a central feature and therefore the scroll in the missing part of the panel would have been a mirror image.

The apse is a slightly irregular semicircle, which is reflected in the shape of the panel, divided radially to develop five compartments and with a flattened semicircle (lunette) at the base, all drawn in simple guilloche. In the lunette is a cantharus from which emerge two dolphins, and traces of a foliate motif, perhaps springing from the base. The cantharus has a heavily gadrooned bowl shaded red, brown and white, with a plain body and a wide mouth. Its handles are mostly obscured by the dolphins whose tails are hidden in the dark grey depth of the cantharus; their bodies are brown, grey and white with red fins. Elsewhere in the apse only dark grey, red and white *tesserae* are used. The five segment-like compartments, framed by a dark grey double fillet, contain highly stylised 'candelabra' surmounted by a circle, with tendrils and leaves; the central and the outside ones have small faces at their bases. The motifs are not well executed and are clumsily twisted to fit the compartment, occasionally intruding into the frame. The southernmost two appear to be different with red interlacing circles edged in dark grey, perhaps by another hand. Surrounding the semicircle is a foliate scroll, similar to that on the chord panel except lacking sheaths, and a coarse red border.

The workmanship displayed in the figured panels is good, but elsewhere the same standard is not maintained and errors abound, leading to the possible conclusions that either the master mosaicist was responsible only for figured work or that the figured compartments were prefabricated. The hunting scene, the foliate scroll and the general scheme point to it being an example of the work of the *Durnovarian* Group but such an attribution is far less certain than with other mosaics here assigned to that group. The figured work, especially where it can best be judged in the antelope and leopard compartment, is exceptionally realistic, and certainly by a different hand from the creatures with their distinctive bulging musculature at Frampton, Hinton St

Mary (Dorset) and Cherhill (Wiltshire). The error in the geometry of Panel A is also exemplified at Frampton and Hinton St Mary, both products of the *Durnovarian* Group, but many mosaics demonstrate errors in layout and on balance the mosaic's attribution to that group is doubtful.

Room 12 (Figure 65)

Found 1972. Dimensions: room 3 x 25m+ (probably at least 30m). *Tesserae*: dark grey, white and red, 20mm; border, grey and brown, 35mm. Post AD 353.

Along the south-east side of the building is a long veranda with a mosaic extending as far as Room 19 where steps lead to a lower flagged area near the baths. Although the south-west end was ploughed out and the north-eastern end unexcavated, it would seem to consist of a continuous panel of simple meander with double returns in dark grey and red on a white ground. It was bound by bands of white, dark grey and white, and by a border of grey with some brown interspersed. One of the elements of the meander is elongated perhaps as a compensation or correction. The design is a more elaborate version of that in Room 6.

Room 25, Mosaic A (colour plate 21)

Found 1974. Dimensions: room 6.10m square. *Tesserae*: dark grey, white, red, yellow and grey, pale grey, 10mm. Fourth century. Preserved in Dorset County Museum.

This is the earlier of the two mosaics from Room 25. (They had both subsided in antiquity and Mosaic A was levelled with hardcore to bed Mosaic B.) The surviving fragment shows the northern corner of the design. The outermost surviving border is a spaced double latchkey-meander executed in dark grey and red on a white ground, the latchkeys being upright on the north-east side and recumbent on the north-west side. The spaces formed are square, of which parts of three survive: one being a guilloche mat with strands alternately shaded in red and white, and grey and white, unusually edged in red; of the other two, traces in the corner may be an inward-pointing heart-shape in one, perhaps part of a stylised flower, while the other has a red pelta, possibly part of a swastika-pelta of unconventional form, both in red linear frames.

Within this is a band of right-angled Z-pattern, with the elements shaded alternately in red, yellow and white, and grey, pale grey and white, enclosing two adjacent panels. In the angle is a spaced swastika-meander with single returns enclosing at least one linear square with a small central square, all in dark grey on a white ground; it is in a rectangular dark grey linear frame with an additional dark grey line on the north-east side. Only a right angle of three-strand guilloche, with two strands in red and white (x2) and one in grey and white (x2), remains of the other panel.

The workmanship is not of a high standard and the design seems to contain several adjustments, such as the extra line in the spaced swastika-meander panel and the changes of colour in the double latchkey-meander, and clumsy cornering in the right-angled Z-pattern and the double latchkey-meander that required a dogleg. The unusual red margin on the guilloche mat and the red frames are matched in Room 11 so it is quite possible the two floors are contemporary, dating to after AD 353. However, otherwise the

65 The strip mosaic from the veranda of the Dewlish Roman Villa

mosaic is of quite different character to others at Dewlish (for instance, in its greater use of colour in repetitive motifs), and the later floor has closer affinities to the others.

Room 25, Mosaic B (colour plate 20)

Found 1974. Dimensions: room 6.10m square. *Tesserae*: dark grey, white, red, brown, dark red and yellow, 18mm; border: red, 25-30mm, 40-45mm. Post AD 353. The greater part is preserved in Dorset County Museum.

A large fragment was discovered in the north corner of the room sealing Mosaic A; three small fragments were found to the south-west. The design appears to comprise a very broad white band, enhanced by a single dark grey fillet near the margins, framing a square or rectangular panel of which only a band of red edged with dark grey forming a right angle remains. The broad white band contains a marine scene of sea-beasts, each outlined in dark grey and shaded brown and white, with tails, fins and streamers in red.

Working anti–clockwise first is the cloven hoof and foreleg of an otherwise lost creature. Forward of and above this is a fierce-looking dolphin with a coiled tail and serrated red streamers. This appears to be chasing a sea-leopard, its head turned to confront the dolphin. It has a gaping mouth, red streamers behind the head, dark grey spots on its forequarters formed by single *tesserae*, forelegs with two elongated and clawed toes, and a coiled body with red excrescences and a tail with three red flukes (only two survive).

At the corner and at right angles to the sea-leopard, which it partly obscures, is a creature with similar hindquarters but with cloven hooves and a head with a curled horn indicative of a sea-ram. It also turns its head to look backwards.

Ahead of the sea-ram is a fragmentary creature that may be connected with the depiction of a 'human' figure of which only the upper body, part of the head and a flying cloak over the right shoulder survive. The figure, perhaps a Cupid riding a sea-creature, is outlined in dark grey and is shaded dark red, yellow and white. Of the other fragments, one shows the foreparts of a creature with the chest and forelegs outlined dark grey and shaded red, yellow, white and with some grey on the body. Directly above this a largely white fragment has loops of dark grey infilled red and a trace of yellow; this seems to be the hair of a human head indicating the rider of the creature or, given its position, the head of a centaur.

A small fragment exists at the threshold of Room 26 showing that fine white tessellation, edged in dark grey, continued through into the room. On the south-east side of the mosaic is a red border of coarse red *tesserae*, which, here at least, is laid unusually with rows at right angles to the wall, with the exception of three rows closest to the panel that are executed in slightly larger *tesserae*. This technique is also noted Room 16. The coarse red tessellation extends beyond the line of the wall in the north corner, indicating an opening to Room 26.

The workmanship is quite good, even though relatively large *tesserae* are employed. The creatures are lively and imaginatively drawn. It clearly postdates Mosaic A below and a tentative date of *c*.AD 370-80 was given by the excavator. It was in use long enough to require a mortar repair to a worn area near the doorway. Panels with sea-creatures are not uncommon, especially in bath-suites for which it is apposite, and are found in south-west Britain, for example from Bath and from Bromham, Wiltshire. However, the only other example in Britain to include cupids or nereids is the second-century example from Dyer Street, Cirencester.

Although this is not a typical product of the *Durnovarian* Group, the black-edged red band is also found at Fifehead Neville, Hemsworth, and Low Ham, Somerset, which are all assignable to it; it also occurs in Room 11. The dolphin, particularly the shape and internal loops, is reminiscent of *Durnovarian* workmanship; it could be a late example of their work or merely shows influence. It is interesting to note that one of the Fifehead Neville mosaics featuring black-edged red bands similarly lacks guilloche work, but the sea-creatures are not comparable.

The Dewlish Villa has been described in some detail, because of its importance and the good state of survival of the main house. Its collection of mosaics is outstanding. It remains to be seen how typical it was of the villas in Dorset generally, and it may be that its conversion into a rural religious centre makes it exceptional.

9

RELIGION IN ROMAN DORSET

The Roman world had many religions, and generally speaking any religion was tolerated by the government provided it obeyed the rules. In particular this meant that it had to allow for the deity of the emperor, and this presented little if any difficulty to the many gods of the Greek and Roman Pantheon (see below).

Christianity of course could not allow the deity of the emperor and this led to the persecution of Christians, particularly under Nero and Diocletian. But Christianity was a very different religion from most of the others, requiring a faith in its one true god and high standards of personal behaviour. Believers were promised rewards in an afterlife.

Following the conversion of the emperor Constantine in AD 312, Christianity became the official and required faith of the Empire. Some of the other religions suffered repression in their turn, but many continued to flourish in far off corners of the Empire.

THE PANTHEON

Until the spread of Christianity, most Romans (and the Greeks before them) worshipped the many and varied gods of the Pantheon. This is difficult for us to understand, since a traditional Roman god was completely unlike most twenty-first-century ideas of God.

The gods were simply a superhuman race, giant in stature, immortal, and living on Mount Olympus or in other magical and inaccessible locations. They lived their own lives and obeyed no moral rules in doing so. They fought, stole and went to bed with the wrong partners. Jupiter was their king and Juno their queen. They all had special attributes, for example Mars, god of war, and Venus, goddess of love and beauty.

The gods were not necessarily concerned with human life at all; they just carried on with their own affairs. But, of course, they were all powerful and could if they wished intervene in human life to considerable effect. Thus it was that enormous sums of money were expended both at public and private level to catch the interest of a god and persuade him or her to intervene in human life.

This was done by the provision of temples, expensive and attractive buildings, which provide some of the very best examples of classical architecture; the Parthenon in Athens was simply the home provided by the Athenians for their patron goddess Athene. You hoped that the god would find your temple irresistibly attractive and reside there. The temple was the god's home and no one was allowed in except the priest or priestess. Assemblies of people, if they happened at all, occurred around an outdoor altar in front of the temple.

Grand ceremonies were carried out at state level, and at a personal level you attracted the god's attention by making offerings of small cakes, wine, small animals or even a bull – the more expensive, the more likely to succeed! Food offerings were consumed by the priests on the god's behalf. The temples were normally surrounded by shops selling offerings for you to make at the temple or providing services such as divination.

Excavations of temples often produce examples of this process, since the wealthy, when successful, recorded their offerings on stone altars which can still be read. The best instance in the province of Britain is at Bath where Sulis, goddess of the hot spring, was worshipped. In the days of primitive medicine those gods which offered healing were most successful in financial terms; this accounts for the great wealth of the buildings in the temple complex at Bath. Bath (*Aquae Sulis*) was not a normal town. The whole complex was given over to the worship of Sulis and the commercial activities connected with it.

DORSET

When the Romans came to Britain they found many gods being worshipped in a similar way to their own. This presented no problem; the gods carried on, and in many cases were declared to be identical with particular Roman gods. For instance Sulis at Bath was equated with Minerva, and is addressed on some inscriptions by the double name.

The only exception was the religion of the Druids. This, we are told, involved human sacrifice and other unmentionable horrors. This was probably true. Druidism was forbidden and the historian Tacitus gives a graphic description of the violent destruction of the priests and their sacred groves on Anglesey, said to be the heart of the cult. We do not know if the Druids operated among the Durotriges, though it is likely enough. But it is almost certain that throughout Dorset local gods existed in a style very similar to the Roman gods; these would have been worshipped at magical spots such as forests and springs.

By the spring at Cerne Abbas is the huge chalk figure of a fertility god (*66*); perhaps in the Cerne Giant we can actually see a picture of a native Durotrigian god, as assimilated into the Roman system. There is, however, an urgent need for scientific tests to be done on the Cerne Giant to confirm his antiquity. There are persuasive arguments that he might belong to a much later period, that of the English Civil War of the seventeenth century.

If the Cerne Abbas figure was that of a Romano–Celtic god, then somewhere on the hillside or more likely under the present village near the spring, will have been a temple and other features associated with his worship.

No doubt with Roman names as well as their own, these gods continued to be worshipped in the countryside. In the towns there will have been greater pressure for

66 The Cerne Giant

allegiance to be transferred to the Roman gods themselves. As we shall see, many of these native gods staged a comeback in the later years of Roman Britain.

CHRISTIANITY

Neither Dorchester nor Ilchester has yet produced a single temple to any god, native or Roman, though no doubt they existed. Oddly enough it is the countryside which has given us some very spectacular evidence. In two Dorset villas the mosaic floors of the

67 The Roman temple at Jordan Hill

main reception-cum-dining room (*triclinium*) contain one of the symbols of Christianity. This was the logo formed from the Greek letters chi and rho, which together represent chr, the first letters of Christ's name.

At Frampton Villa, 5 miles west of Dorchester in the valley of the Frome, the main pavement (see *49*) featured figures from classical mythology, including Cupid, Neptune, and the story of Bellerephon and the Chimaera. Neptune and Cupid are honoured in lines of verse set into the floor. But very oddly the dining apse (if that is what it is) which opens from the main room has on its threshold three floral whorls on either side of a roundel containing the chi-rho symbol.

It raises intriguing but unanswerable questions. Was the owner Christian? If so, what is Neptune doing so prominently elsewhere on the floor? Was the side-room used as a Christian chapel and its use symbolised in the floor as you entered? Perhaps Neptune and the other ancient gods were regarded as mere figures of mythology, not seen to be in conflict with Christianity? Nevertheless in several parts of the room pictures of mythological scenes have at some time been hacked from the floor, and this may be the work of Christians who felt they were inappropriate.

At Hinton St Mary near Sturminster Newton (see *51*), the pictures are less equivocal. Bellerophon and the Chimaera appear in the apse, but the central panel in the main room shows the head and shoulders of a man; behind him is the chi-rho symbol, and on either side pomegranates, symbols of eternal life. There is very little doubt that this is meant to be Christ. As such it is a floor of the greatest importance, and it is not surprising that it was purchased by the British Museum. (The pavements at Frampton are buried again, and may have been severely damaged by the construction of water meadows.)

These mosaic floors, taken together with evidence from Dorchester, at least confirm that in the fourth century AD (if not before) Christianity had come to Dorset and was probably widespread. In the cemetery at Poundbury outside Dorchester upwards of 1000 burials were found, aligned in Christian fashion and the bodies fully extended on their backs (see *29*). The manner of burial coupled with the absence of grave goods, and the occasional find of a chi-rho coin pierced for wearing round the neck, indicate that this was one of the burial places of the Christian community in *Durnovaria*.

There was probably a church in the town, similar to the small one known from Silchester. Moreover, in the Poundbury cemetery among the graves were several mausolea. In one of these fragments of painted wall decoration show rows of officials with staffs of office, perhaps church elders (*colour plate 9*). The decoration includes one chi-rho.

Other finds from Dorset confirm the practice of Christianity. These include two silver rings from the villa at Fifehead Neville with chi-rho on the bezel and a group of silver spoons found at Somerleigh Court in Dorchester. One of these has a fish depicted on the bowl, and another the message *Augustine vivas*, both indicating Christian use. The spoons, found with 50 silver coins, may well have been part of the ritual of the Dorchester church, buried in some emergency and never recovered.

PAGAN GODS

The major evidence for the revival of pagan religion at the end of the Roman period lies in three Romano-Celtic temples, one at Jordan Hill, near Weymouth, one at Maiden Castle and one newly discovered at Badbury Rings. Between them they provide at least an outline picture of the Romanised worship of the pagan gods in the territory of the Durotriges.

JORDAN HILL

Jordan Hill is much damaged and was badly excavated; nevertheless some extraordinary features were recorded and are worth describing in detail.

The temple and a cemetery were found on the hill-crest about 46m above sea level overlooking Weymouth Bay. The building (see *67*) was excavated by J. Medhurst in 1843, and by C.S. Prideaux and C.D. Drew in 1931-2; the exposed foundations (SY 6989 8207) are on permanent display. The cemetery to the north and north-east was investigated by Medhurst in 1845-6.

The temple (*68*) was some 25ft square internally with walls 3ft 8in wide on foundations 9.5ft wide. Both stone and clay roofing tiles were found. A thin concrete surround on all sides was at least 11ft wide on the south and 9ft on the west. Observers in 1843, perhaps misled by two offsets in the foundations, noted traces of steps at the centre of the south wall. Bases of four small columns *in situ* 4ft from it, a limestone base and a Purbeck marble Tuscan capital for a column or columns about 5ft high (in Dorset County Museum) were found loose near the north wall.

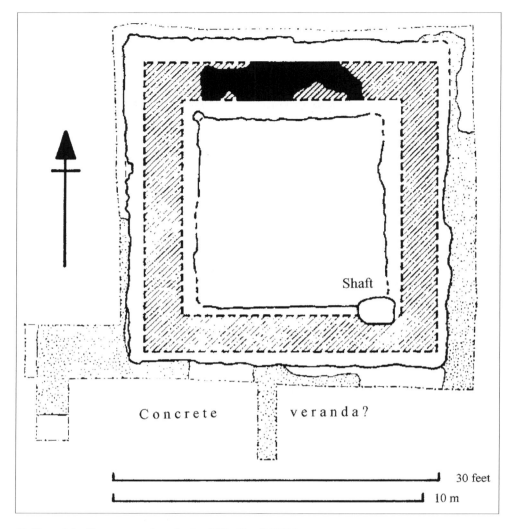

68 Plan of the Roman temple at Jordan Hill. *After RCHM*

An oblong shaft 4 x 3ft and 12ft deep lay within the south-east angle, largely under the line of the wall footings; the sides were lined with roofing slabs set in clay, and the filling consisted of 16 layers of ash and charcoal alternating with double layers of roofing slabs arranged in superimposed pairs, between each of which were bones of a single bird and a small bronze coin. At the bottom a stone cist contained two urns, a sword, spear-head, knife, steelyard, bucket-handle, crook and other iron objects; a similar cist half-way down enclosed urns, a sword and a spear-head. The bird bones were identified as of buzzard, raven, starling and crow, and one coin as of Theodosius I (379-95). There were also bones of a hare.

The building was set, apparently centrally, in an outer square enclosure, not confirmed in 1931-2, with walls 5ft thick and dimensions variously given as 280ft square, 110ft or

37yds square. This would give the standard pattern of a Romano-Celtic temple, a square shrine within a square veranda.

Within this area were found many animal remains, especially horns of oxen, pottery, and about 300 coins all apparently of the late Empire including one of Arcadius (383-408). In later excavations and consolidation 177 coins were found on the site, 61 of them certainly of the period 388-95, amongst them a bronze Durotrigian coin and examples from Vespasian (69-79) to Arcadius. Of two coin hoards discovered on the hill, one in 1812 consisted of several hundred silver coins, mostly it seems of 244-68; the other, found in 1928, was of over 4400 bronze coins ranging from Postumus (259-68) to Honorius (393-423) but mostly issued after 379.

The cemetery, perhaps pre-Roman in origin, lay north and north-east and extended at least 300yds over an area where Roman material occurs on the surface. The most reliable account is probably that of T.W. Wake Smart in Warne's *Ancient Dorset*. About 80 inhumation burials of adults and children were found in an area of about 1 acre, variously orientated and often flexed, and sometimes in groups of up to six individuals.

Some were in stone cists and one grave was paved with chalk *tesserae*; nails indicated that some had been in wooden coffins. Low dry-stone walls, one of crescent-shape 21ft long, apparently demarcated burial plots and sometimes had burials in their structure (Shipp (in Hutchins) states that the cemetery was within a parallelogram 500ft across with a low thick wall). Near the burials were (i) several floors of white clay, one seemingly of 18 x 12ft with stone walls; (ii) clay-lined hollows containing ashes, animal bones and sherds, several apparently provided with stone-lined drains; (iii) two stone cists containing burnt shale and calcined animal bones; (iv) several stone piles on which rested animal bones or vessels containing them.

Some burials had single pots or groups; in one group of nine vessels, three (a samian dish, a black ware imitation of samian form 37 and a handled cup of black ware) stood on an engraved oblong plaque or tray of shale placed at the shoulder, with five black ware bowls ranged around it, and a bottle of yellowish ware at the knees. Another imitation of samian form 37 was made of shale. Some 80 vessels survive, mostly in Dorset County Museum and the British Museum, out of perhaps 125 listed as from Jordan Hill in sale catalogues of the Medhurst Collection (Sotheby's, 1 July 1879; C.T. Jefferies, Bristol, 1893).

The picture this gives of the ritual practised in a Romano-Celtic temple in the late fourth century is extraordinary. In particular the deep shaft with its strange fill is difficult to parallel or understand. The popularity of the site and the wealth expended were considerable. It should however be remembered that in sites such as this archaeology can only pick up the outward signs of religious practices through structures and artefacts found. Faith, fervour, music, language and fashion can only be guessed at.

MAIDEN CASTLE

The Maiden Castle temple was excavated by Wheeler (*69*), and a full account can be read in his report on the hillfort. The temple consisted of a square *cella* or shrine, surrounded

69 The Roman temple in Maiden Castle under excavation in 1938. © *Dorset Natural History and Archaeological Society*

by a square portico, as at Jordan Hill. This was the usual shape in the third and fourth centuries for temples of native gods, as distinct from the classical Roman ones, who are more likely to have had classical temples with columns and decorated pediment.

Beside the Maiden Castle temple lay a small two-roomed house, presumably for the priest and the offices. There is some evidence that all the eastern end of the hillfort was walled off to form the temple precinct. It seems to have been reasonably prosperous, but we have no means of knowing the name of the god. The date of construction was again in the second half of the fourth century AD.

Most interesting of all is the fact that below the ruins of the temple (which can still be seen) Wheeler found a small wooden hut from the hillfort of 400 years before the temple, and this hut may itself have been a shrine. It is possible that one of the gods of the Durotriges, worshipped in the old hillfort, had retained his/her identity, to benefit from a pagan revival in the late fourth century.

Certainly there was a pagan revival at this time and one wonders what the Christian community thought of it. In some parts of Britain such temples became extremely prosperous and the best-known example is at Lydney in Gloucestershire, also excavated by Wheeler.

BADBURY RINGS

The Badbury Rings temple lay immediately south-west of the great hillfort, beside the Roman road to Dorchester. Passers-by on the road could not fail to see the building in its eight-sided enclosure.

The site has been very severely damaged and for many years treasure-hunters were known to have removed numerous coins and possibly other artefacts from the site. This led to an excavation organised by Martin Papworth for the National Trust in the year 2000, to assess the damage and discover what information could still be recovered from the site. There was very little left, and archaeological features only survived where they had cut into the natural chalk.

The central square temple was of the usual pattern of a 15m-square shrine within a 3m-wide veranda, confirming the identification of the site. Unusually it lay within an eight-sided enclosure or *temenos*. Towards the southern edge of this enclosure lay traces of another rectangular building, which may well have been the priest's house or offices.

Nothing was found to give a clue as to the identity of the god worshipped here, but in view of its proximity to the old hillfort, it is quite likely that, as at Maiden Castle, a native god saw a revival of fortune late in the Roman period.

DEWLISH

At the villa at Dewlish (see chapter 8) the late fourth century saw the building of a small square temple and an attendant house; this too may have been for a Celtic god, but heavy ploughing has removed any certain evidence.

10

INDUSTRY IN ROMAN DORSET

One of the attractions which brought the Romans to Britain was the prospect of profits from a variety of industries. The first-century geographer Strabo described pre-Roman Britain as exporting gold, silver, iron, slaves, corn, cattle, hides and hunting dogs. Mines for the various metals became the personal property of the emperor and run for his private profit by procurators. These mines provided some of the few instances in Roman Britain where industry operated on the large, messy scale more familiar to us from the Industrial Revolution.

The most famous of these is perhaps the gold mine at Dolaucothi in Central Wales, with its multiple aqueducts supplying water power. Similar scenes could be found at the lead and silver mines of Charterhouse, the tin mines of Cornwall, the iron mines of the Weald, and other mining centres.

No metal was mined in Dorset, but there were two major and no doubt profitable industries: stone and pottery. The pottery industry was almost certainly in private Durotrigian hands, while the stone industries may have had local or just possibly imperial owners.

POTTERY

In the cemeteries found at Maiden Castle the dead were buried with a variety of pottery bowls to provide food for their journey to another world. These pots included distinctive shallow bowls known to archaeologists as war-cemetery bowls. Along with most of the other pottery found at Maiden Castle, they were made by a thriving prehistoric pottery industry based in Purbeck and using the ball-clays and sands from the tertiary deposits north of the chalk ridge. In fact the distribution of this pottery is one of the ways in which the territory of the Durotriges is defined. Some pots were exported to the continent, and examples have been found as far away as Bordeaux.

The Durotrigian potters made distinctive bowls, plates, cups, cooking pots and jugs, produced without the aid of a wheel, and finished by burnishing the surface with a bone polisher. The pots were fired in clamps often without the use of permanent kilns. During

70 Black Burnished Ware pots from Dorchester

the final stages of firing air was excluded, resulting in a black or grey finish to the pots. In many cases a black slip was also applied. There are cases where an area of a pot has accidentally fired white or orange and has then been carefully blacked over after firing to achieve the expected black finish.

When the Roman army arrived it is clear that the vigorous pottery industry saw its commercial chance. Within a year or two of its arrival the Second Augustan Legion was using Durotrigian pottery of most types in its camps for cooking purposes. It imported samian and other fine wares from Gaul for table use.

As the years passed and the army moved on to the Midlands, Wales, and finally the northern frontiers, the Durotrigian salesmen followed and continued to get the contracts. Other purchases were made of course, but in a typical excavation on Hadrian's Wall, for instance, over 50 per cent of the coarse pottery found will be from the Durotrigian industry. Many boats must have sailed from Poole Harbour laden with the products, on their journey to the harbour at South Shields near Newcastle and other northern harbours.

At first the traditional Durotrigian shapes were produced. But gradually the potters were influenced by the requirements of their new customers and new shapes appeared, particularly cooking pots, flange-rimmed bowls and pie dishes (70).

Amazingly the potters did not change their methods of working. They did not change over to using wheels, and many continued to fire in temporary clamps, though kilns

71 A Black Burnished Ware kiln from the Bestwall excavations

were also introduced. Similarly they continued to burnish the pots, with a little token decoration in the form of incised wavy and/or diagonal lines.

Not surprisingly this pottery is known to archaeologists as Black Burnished Ware (for a review of the products of this industry see Woodward 1993 p.229ff). The proof that the pottery on Hadrian's Wall was identical to that found in Dorchester was one of the early triumphs of the scientific approach to archaeology. It was done at Southampton University by the examination of thin sections of pottery under the microscope; this proved that the minerals present in the pots found in the north could only have come from Purbeck.

One of the outstanding excavations of recent years has been that conducted by Lilian Ladle at Bestwall Quarry immediately east of Wareham (see www.bestwall.co.uk). Among many important discoveries belonging to many periods of Dorset history, kilns (71) and working areas of the Black Burnished Ware industry were found.

In this particular location (there were undoubtedly many others) the pottery industry flourished from c.AD 200 till perhaps as late as AD 450. Some 32 kiln-type structures were found. These were in four distinct types:

Type 1: thick, clay-lined ovens with stoke flues and large stoke pits
Type 2: thin-walled ovens of clay, sometimes with secondary chambers to the rear or side
Type 3: rectangular stone ovens with a stoke pit but no flue
Type 4: small ephemeral clay and stone ovens with large amounts of charcoal present.

It is not possible to be certain whether these belong to different dates, or merely the habits of different operators. The kilns occur in small ditched fields. Vast quantities of pottery have been recovered, including pots which were abandoned in collapsed kilns. All the known and documented forms of Black Burnished Ware were found on the site, suggesting that individual potters did not specialise in the types they produced.

There were also 18 clay pits, 9 lean-to workshops and a water hole. There was evidence that one building was used for clay preparation and another for storing prepared clay. A circular wooden hut with a fire in the centre was possibly used for drying the pots before firing, but there was also a stone-built drying kiln, constructed like the corn-dryers (or possibly barley-malters) often found on late villa sites.

Artefacts found included 26 stone burnishers and curved templates to shape the inside of pots. There was kiln furniture to help support the pots during firing, though this was missing from kilns of the fourth century, suggesting less professional working. Overall this remarkable excavation has provided a new and clear insight into the workings of perhaps the largest pottery industry in Roman Britain.

An industry that also made use of Dorset clay was brick and tile. Almost every Roman site produces quantities of *tegula* and *imbrex*, the familiar Roman clay-tiled roof elements. Square tiles for hypocausts are frequently found, and other less usual items such as the antefixes (roof ornaments) from Dorchester (*colour plate 25*).

However, no brick and tile works has so far been located in Dorset. It may be that the kilns were temporary structures made by the builders for specific projects and leaving comparatively little trace. An example of specific production for one building is the tile from Dorchester stamped NVND (*72*). This may stand for *Nundinae*, a market held every nine days. The tiles were made for the building and stamped to ensure they were not stolen or allocated to other uses. The stamp would not have been visible when built into the structure. The legions normally stamped their tile production, but none are known from Dorset.

STONE

The stone found in Roman buildings in Dorset came from a variety of quarries. Dressed stone in the Dewlish villa and coffins from the Poundbury cemetery were made of hamstone from Ham Hill, near Ilminster (*59*). Some Chilmark stone appears at Dewlish also (Chilmark is in Wiltshire). Portland stone was extensively used for buildings and particularly for fourth-century coffins on the island. But the most active industry appears to have been in Purbeck, where a variety of stone types were quarried.

Limestone from various beds was used for almost every building purpose, from quoins to roof tiles. Thousands of diamond-pattern stone tiles have been found on Roman sites in Dorset, and the recently restored Roman town house in Dorchester has been roofed with new 'Roman' stone tiles from the same quarries as the originals.

More specialised was Purbeck marble. This is a shelly limestone which can be cut and polished to a high degree – it has been used in more recent times, and can be seen for

72 A tile from Dorchester stamped NVND[INAE], probably referring to the nine-day market.
© *Wessex Archaeology*

example in the columns of Salisbury Cathedral. Much of the marble appears to have been quarried away in the Middle Ages, so it is not clear where the Roman quarries were, but one may have been at Wilkswood, near Langton Matravers.

It was moved surprising distances in Roman Britain and has been found as far away as London and Chester. It was mainly used for finely dressed stone, especially inscriptions. The famous inscription from Chichester mentioning the name of Cogidubnus is of Purbeck marble, showing that this industry (which does not seem to have existed before the Romans) had developed early in the history of Roman Britain. No doubt the Roman taste for marble generated a search in likely areas for a substitute. A temple dedication slab at Verulamium is made of Purbeck marble, as is the tombstone of Carinus at Dorchester.

One unusual industry was based on Kimmeridge shale. This bituminous shale is found at Kimmeridge Bay and had been worked in prehistoric times. It can be burnt as fuel, but more particularly, when newly quarried, can be worked almost like wood, especially on a lathe. It was then polished to a high-gloss black finish. Its uses included the manufacture of bangles, beads, plates, dishes, bowls, and furniture including tables and chairs (see *25*). There were also decorated trays and architectural features such as wall panels and mosaic *tesserae*. The cold plunge bath at Dewlish Villa was lined with slabs of Kimmeridge shale (*73*), and this material too was widely traded across Britain.

For many years archaeologists found the small round cores removed by the lathe when making bangles and these caused much puzzling over their purpose, until it was realised

73 Kimmeridge shale sheets lining the cold plunge bath at the Dewlish Roman Villa

they were simply a waste product. The cores are found on many sites, including most of the villas, indicating that slabs of Kimmeridge shale were bought in bulk for local manufacture of bangles and other items.

OTHER INDUSTRIES

The pottery and stone industries achieved province-wide success. More locally the supply of timber and charcoal was important throughout Dorset. It is difficult to underestimate the importance of the forests and wooden products. Many houses were built of timber, and timber was used extensively in the roofs even of buildings otherwise made of stone or brick.

Road vehicles were wooden. Fuel for heating and industrial processes was entirely wood. Charcoal was needed in quantity for industrial smelting of metals. Most household fittings and tools, now of plastic, were of wood. A spectacular museum in this connection is that at *Vindolanda* south of Hadrian's Wall. Here a large waterlogged deposit has preserved an extraordinary collection of wooden objects, and any study of carpentry in Roman Britain starts there. It is of course most famous for its remarkable collection of wooden writing tablets, which reveal so much detail about life on the northern frontier.

None of this survives in Dorset, except rarely in wet layers at the bottom of a well. Nevertheless wood will have been a most significant resource. It may not be too fanciful to imagine a 'Wood resources committee' (the author wonders if it might have been called the *Concilium Durnovariense ad silvas administrandas*) meeting in Dorchester to allocate licences for forest use. There is no evidence for such a body, but aerial photography has shown how much of Dorset was under plough and the remaining forested area will have been very valuable.

Crystallisation of salt from sea water occurred at a number of places along the coast, especially on the shores of Poole harbour. The evidence for this is 'briquetage', the pottery pans used for the process. A whole range of industries were related to farming (for which see chapter 6), including leather working. Cloaks made from British wool (the *Birrus Britannicus*) were famous as far afield as Rome, and no doubt some came from Dorset.

In the towns there will have been an enormous number of small establishments providing services and products made on the premises, from butchers and greengrocers to metalworkers of every sort. A time traveller to Roman Dorset would find a complex pattern of trade not all that dissimilar to that of the nineteenth century.

An excavation in the 1960s in the garden of Somerleigh Court in Dorchester discovered a building remarkably similar to a 'unit' on a modern industrial estate (74). Different trades were active in different parts of the building. There were the stokeholes (75) of furnaces, though it is always difficult to discover exactly what the furnace was being used for. One unusual find (76) was a large water jar set into the floor, perhaps for quenching iron. It still had its stone cover in position.

74 Industrial workshops in Somerleigh Court in Dorchester

75 Stokehole for a furnace in Somerleigh Court in Dorchester

76 A large pot set into the floor in a workshop in Somerleigh Court, Dorchester

However, all the industries relied entirely on manual labour, and there were no labour laws such as we have today. Individual workers will have suffered from the effects of market forces, political and military disasters, good and bad harvests and other such problems. Many workers will have been slaves, and the quality of their life will have depended as much on their masters or mistresses as on the wider trading situation. Our understanding of working conditions in the Roman world is as yet very limited.

It is surprising how close the Romans came to the inventions of the Industrial Revolution. The power of steam was understood in principle, but the technology to make use of it was never achieved except in small experiments. The mass smelting of iron ore and the production of cast iron was not achieved at all. Fans of Adam Hart-Davis and his programmes entitled *What did the Romans do for us?* will have seen reconstructions of some of the remarkable inventions they constructed.

11

THE ROMAN ROADS

Think of the Romans and their roads come first to mind. The Romans did not invent roads. Many of the preceding civilisations in the Middle East had them, but it was the Romans who developed them into the comprehensive system on which the administration of their Empire depended. Naturally the system penetrated Dorset.

Before the Romans came to Britain there were no roads at all, at least in the meaning of an engineered route with hard surface, foundations, drainage and bridges. There were of course trackways resulting from the passage of travellers; these trackways followed natural routes, and some of them, particularly the ridgeways, went for many miles. In some cases it seems that the Romans built roads which more or less followed the routes of these trackways.

The roads were one of the most drastic landscape changes that the Romans brought. All previous landscape features, even if man-made, were largely controlled by the presence of forests, rivers and hills. Now the route from A to B was in all probability a straight line drawn by an engineer on a map, and surveyed and carried out on the ground, initially at least, by the army. If your house unfortunately lay in its path, no planning permission or compulsory purchase order was needed for its destruction. Initially the roads were built for military purposes; later they were adapted for the use of the new *civitates* and a few new ones built for the purpose.

It is usually difficult to date the construction of a road. In a town, features can be dated from pottery and coins in the buried layers; however, once a road is out in the country miles of it might be excavated without finding anything to help date it. The only cases where it can be done with some certainty are those where a road clearly leads to the gate of a fort, rather than a town.

CONSTRUCTION

Roman roads were straight except where the terrain prevented it; if necessary they zig-zagged on steep descents and even performed long gentle curves. Although visitors to Rome admire the Via Appia, constructed of huge lava blocks, and other similar paved

77 Ackling Dyke, the Roman road on Oakley Down

roads, it must be remembered that the money for this sort of thing was rarely, if ever, available in Britain. British roads were of gravel (*via glareata* in Latin). There are just one or two possible cases of a paved road, and even these are doubtful, though the streets of major cities such as London and Cirencester may have had paved streets, at least in their centres.

After removal of turf and topsoil, larger stones were laid as a foundation. Finer gravel was then added as a running surface. The famous Roman road on Wheeldale Moor in Yorkshire often causes surprise to visitors as the gravel surface has been removed, leaving only the large stones which appear to provide a very bumpy surface. Occasionally kerb stones were used at the road edge, but this is not common in Britain. It seems to have happened when the ditch was close to the road edge, to prevent the gravel filling the ditch as traffic passed, and a good example is the extraordinary road which runs north from the Roman fort at Caersws in Montgomeryshire to Bala. However, in Dorset the ditches are usually well away from the road, often by as much as 4m.

At each side lay a drainage ditch and the road itself was normally carried on a causeway which can in some cases be surprisingly high (particularly Ackling Dyke in Dorset); nevertheless the reason was the same, namely drainage. Nothing destroys a road faster than water and frost. In hollows, culverts carried surface water or streams beneath the road.

The roads were surprisingly narrow; although the causeway (or *agger* in Latin) may have been as much as 20m in width, the running surface at its top was rarely more than 3m (10ft) wide (*77*). This was just enough for two vehicles moving slowly to pass. When traffic ruts survive (*78*) they are normally central on the road. Once a road has been

78 Ackling Dyke passing under Dorchester en route to the Roman fort. Note the traffic ruts

ploughed over it gives the appearance of having been much wider; but this is an illusion caused by the spreading of the *agger*.

Where streams were substantial and the road important, bridges were built, sometimes of stone, sometimes of timber. But if the stream was unlikely to hinder traffic, then a ford was often enough. No Roman bridge survives in Britain, in spite of many traditions to this effect. Normally in Britain rivers have eaten away even the foundations, and roads usually disappear as they enter a river's flood plain. Some idea of what the bridges looked like can be got from surviving examples on the continent such as Sommières, not far from Nîmes. The foundations of bridges on Hadrian's Wall at Chesters and Willowford also give an idea of the structures that once stood there. Responsibility for maintenance of the roads, which initially was carried out by the army, was transferred to the local communities as soon as possible.

NAMES AND MILESTONES

Roman roads normally carried names, and usually commemorated the name of the consul or emperor under whom construction or repair was carried out. However, we do not know the name of any Roman road in Britain, and they may not have had names. Although we are familiar with Watling Street, the Fosse Way, Stane Street and Ackling Dyke, these are Saxon names. Whether they bear any resemblance to what the Romans might have called them is unclear.

79 The Roman milestone from Alington Avenue, Dorchester. © *Wessex Archaeology*

Roads were normally equipped with milestones. These served two purposes: first to remind people of the emperor's name and titles, and second to tell you how far it was to the next fort or town. Occasionally the distance measurements are missing, making it clear that the propaganda function was very important.

There is only one inscribed milestone in Dorset (79), it is possible that an uninscribed stone just outside Dorchester (SY 708 913) may have been one.

A weathered and somewhat battered inscribed Roman milestone, made of Purbeck limestone, was found in the rubble infill of an oven during the excavations in the 1980s at Alington Avenue in Fordington. The milestone, which can be seen in Dorset County Museum, is now 0.55m high, 0.23m wide at the top, and 0.35m wide at the bottom. Some flakes of stone have been broken from the left side but do not disturb the start lines of the text. The top has suffered some damage but is more or less complete. The sloping right-hand side is original and shows regular tooling marks. The bottom alone is a broken edge. The back is smoothly rounded, but not regularly enough for it to have been part of a column drum.

The front has been roughly smoothed, setting-out lines inscribed, and letters cut which at times overlap the setting-out line. There are four lines of text, the first three complete. The single letter visible in the final line is not complete. It could be C, G or S. From the Margam parallel (see below) it is likely to be G, but it is not clear what it means. Postumus was not a joint ruler. The text reads:

IMP | POSTV | MO AVG | G
Imp(eratori) Postumo Aug(usto) <G>
[dedicated] to the Emperor Postumus Augustus

The emperor's titles are in a very abbreviated form. If there was any further text on the missing bottom portion, it may have been a figure giving the mileage and name of a town. How frustrating this is! It might have said 1 mile to *Durnovaria*, and would have confirmed that Dorchester was *Durnovaria* and the spelling of the name. It is frustrating to think that the stump carrying these details is probably still in the ground somewhere.

The closest parallel for the Alington milestone is one from Margam, West Glamorgan (*RIB* 2255), which shows a similar lettering style. That milestone reads:

IMPC | MCL | POS | OAV | GG
Imp(eratori) C(aesari) M(arco) C(assiano) L(atinio) Postumo Aug(usto) <G>

Postumus rebelled against the emperor Gallienus in *c*.AD 260 and formed an independent Gallic Empire consisting of Gaul, Spain and Britain. The Alington milestone probably dates to between *c*.AD 260–69.

Other milestones dedicated to Postumus have been found in Wales and Cornwall. Most of these in fact date to the third century and may reflect renewed activity in quarrying and mining, and hence transport provision. It is conceivable that the Alington

Avenue milestone also reflects a similar provision for the renewal of quarrying in the Purbeck area, coinciding with the rebuilding of the urban centres and their defences. However, as the milestone is broken and reused it is also possible that it came from one of the better-known roads which issued from the gates of *Durnovaria*.

ROADS IN DORSET

Five routes are known for certain in Dorset, and they are described below. Some others have been claimed, but not proved. There may well have been minor routes, particularly to the industries of Purbeck, but these are not likely to have been constructed in the grand manner of Ackling Dyke, and very little trace survives.

A well-known book by the late Norman Field (Field 1992) claimed a large number of other Roman roads in Dorset, but the present author does not accept the authenticity of any of these. The confirmed Roman roads of Dorset are as follows:

1 Old Sarum–Badbury–Lake Farm–Hamworthy

This is the original supply road of the Second Augustan Legion when it first established the fort at Lake Farm and its harbour connection to Hamworthy. Ultimately it came from London, via Staines, Silchester (near Reading) and Old Sarum (near Salisbury). It is aligned on Badbury and almost touches the ramparts as it swings towards Lake Farm. It was built in its very impressive style right from the start, as excavations (see below) have shown no trace of a more modest construction buried beneath it.

It is called Ackling Dyke as it crosses Cranborne Chase, and the name is often applied to other parts of the route. The road enters modern Dorset at Bokerley Junction, where it passes through Bokerley Dyke (SU 033 198). From here it runs straight to Badbury Rings, with one very small change in alignment near Gussage St Michael. Most of the stretch from Gussage to Badbury can be walked, and is one of the most magnificent stretches of undamaged Roman road in Britain.

The road crosses the Stour to reach the fort at Lake Farm (see chapter 2), and then continues south to Hamworthy (at about SZ 005 902), where finds strongly suggest an invasion harbour. It follows that the road was primarily built to bring supplies ashore from the *Classis Britannica* (British Fleet) operating in the Channel. It is difficult to say whether the road continued in use after the military phase was over, but possibly not.

2 Badbury–Weymouth

Once the Roman conquest had moved west to the extent that the area of Dorchester and Weymouth was secure and the Dorchester fort was being planned, the next stage of road building began. A junction immediately north of Badbury Rings (*80*) was installed, and Ackling Dyke extended towards Dorchester.

The route is almost straight to the crossing of the Frome at Dorchester except for a slight change of direction east of West Kingston. It is interesting to speculate whether this change in alignment (and the similar bend at Gussage St Michael) reflects slight

80 The Roman road junction at Badbury Rings

inaccuracies in surveying, or whether they avoid obstacles we are unaware of. In Puddletown Forest (SY 735 923) there is a sharp S-bend in the road; the reason is clear, the road negotiates a steep slope and changes direction temporarily to ease the gradient. The gradient here is approximately 1 in 7, and this may have been the ruling gradient adhered to by the builders.

Excavations on Roman roads tend to produce very little information, especially where the road has been reduced by ploughing. But two excavations were carried out by the former Dorset Institute of Higher Education on Ackling Dyke, at points where it is in perfect condition, and give an indication of what it was like when it was built. One was in Thorncombe Wood (SY 727 920), and one on section 3 of the Dorset roads near Eggardon hillfort (see below); the excavations produced almost identical cross sections.

In Thorncombe Wood the road is on sand and gravel, and its *agger* is built of gravel dug from pits close to the road. The causeway is 8m wide at the base, narrowing at the top to a little over 3m (10ft). Central ruts are still visible on the surface. A section (*colour plate 24*) was cut by students of Weymouth College of Education in July 1968, at SY 7270 9201 near Thomas Hardy's cottage in Higher Bockhampton, about 3.5 km east of Dorchester.

The road drops towards Dorchester at an average gradient of 1 in 9 through a small dry gulley, from the western edge of the Reading Beds of sand and gravel which form Duddle Heath. The road runs onto the Chalk as it leaves the wood and agriculture has almost obliterated it. It forms a very prominent *agger* for some 200m, lying half-way up the north slope of the gulley.

The excavation took place 135m into the wood from its western boundary (measuring along the road), in an area covered in a dense growth of birch, gorse and bracken. Preliminary work was done by Drott excavator. Then a 1m strip of the road surface was cleared on the east half of the cross section, and a 2m cutting taken through the road to the natural on the west side (*colour plate 24*). The section was a total length of 17m.

The road was made of orange gravel with small patches of sand and clay, stained brown where it lies within 30cm of the present surface. A number of hollows in the wooded slope immediately north of the road are probably the source of the material. Little more than the turf had been removed from the original ground before laying the road. At the uphill (northern) edge of the carriageway the road gravel was 0.25m thick, while at the downhill edge it was 0.50m. There was a probable marking-out trench visible on the south side, immediately under the southern edge of the running surface. The total width of the *agger* was 7m.

Only leaf-soil and a tangle of roots overlay the Roman surface and two wheel tracks were clearly visible, with centres about 1.5m apart. From the surface of the carriageway the sides of the *agger* sloped at an angle of about 25°. Owing to the angle of the ground on which the road is built, the southern side slope consists entirely of road metalling, while the northern slope is actually cut into the natural subsoil, the upper layer of which is a soft grey sand. This, coupled with absence of flints rolled down from the southern slope, suggests that the sides of the *agger* were turfed at the time of construction; had this not been done, the north side would have eroded away in the first heavy rain. No doubt the result was very like the forestry roads of today which can be seen in Puddletown Forest to the east.

On the south (downhill) side of the *agger* it is remarkable that hardly a single stone has rolled down the hill from the road. There was no ditch within the trench excavated; the dip in the surface of the natural orange gravel which occurs 2m from the southern end of the trench is a natural feature, being circular in plan. The surface of this gravel is easily felt by a probe, and systematic probing beyond the end of the trench indicated that there was no ditch. This is not surprising, as on a slope with a naturally draining subsoil a ditch would serve no useful purpose.

On the north (uphill) side, again no ditch was found up to the end of the trench, at which point the natural slope resumed and a ditch became impossible. There are many changes of colour in the subsoil here, but these are a natural feature of the Reading Beds. Water presumably ran, if at all, in the dip between the road and the hillside. It is worthy of note that where the road reaches the crest of the ridge 450m to the east on level ground, it is equipped with ditches and external side-banks, measuring about 35m across the whole. This suggests that ditches exist for drainage, and side-banks to dispose of material unsuited for use in the *agger*.

The gravel of which the road was built showed no stratification. The small patches of clay and sand within the gravel were carefully examined and found to be chance patches quarried with the gravel, rather than ruts or potholes of earlier surfaces. It is difficult if not impossible to avoid the conclusion that the road is of one build with no sign of repair. This is confirmed by the absence of debris from heavy traffic and wear down the southern slope.

This is surprising in a road, with a presumed life of more than 300 years, which was apparently the main route from London to Dorchester and Exeter. Perhaps this overestimates the amount of land traffic. Water transport was extensively used and loads of pottery from as close as Purbeck and the New Forest probably went by sea to both towns. On the other hand the road as excavated has the air of an expensive prestige road which proved a white elephant and had little use. Since the road was constructed with such a high *agger* and such steep sides, it would have in any case been difficult for local post-military traffic to gain access to the road surface except at the towns and road junctions. Much fieldwork remains to be done before we fully understand the road system of the south-west.

At Dorchester the road crossed the Frome and ran to the new fort site, somewhere on the south-west side of the town. Passing Maumbury Rings (at this time in process of transformation into an amphitheatre) it continued to Weymouth to connect once more with the fleet in the Channel. Unlike the Hamworthy road, it is reasonably certain that this road will have continued in use to serve the civilian town of *Durnovaria* after the departure of the army from the south.

The location of the harbour in Weymouth is quite uncertain, in spite of the tradition that it was at the village of Radipole. Firstly the coastline and sea levels have changed drastically since Roman times, making it difficult to establish the nature of the Backwater and the River Wey in the first century AD. Secondly, although some finds have been made at Radipole, these only reflect settlement and not necessarily a harbour; finds have equally come from elsewhere, including some from the Backwater itself, near the gasholder. Thirdly, the road itself cannot at present be traced further south than the Ridgeway, and so leaves its destination uncertain.

The finds from the Backwater include a complete amphora which presumably fell overboard during unloading, and might suggest that this was the location of the Roman harbour. It is of course possible that the harbour did not require major works such as quaysides. Ships are easily unloaded by coming in on the tide, settling on the bottom as the tide goes out, and floating off on the next tide.

But north of the Ridgeway (*81*) the line of the road is clear, as it now forms the A354 Dorchester–Weymouth road. The route is actually that of the turnpike road, but when trenches are cut in the adjacent fields the side ditches of the preceding Roman road can be seen. Traditionally the road descended over the Ridgeway along the minor road which passes the Ship Inn (SY 670 850), but observation of the fields between the minor road and the turnpike have shown that the Roman road has been ploughed away within the fields some 40–50m west of the turnpike.

3   Dorchester–Exeter

By a date somewhere in the mid-AD 50s the Second Augustan Legion had established a new base at Exeter (*Isca*). Its trunk road was then extended west from a junction near or at the Dorchester fort. The road is much less straight, climbing soon after it leaves the town onto a ridge where it may have followed a prehistoric route. There are many

81 View from the Ridgeway towards Dorchester showing the turnpike on the line of the Roman road from Weymouth harbour

short changes of direction. At SY 577 937 it passed through the east gate of an Iron Age fortified enclosure (*82*). At SY 544 937 it passed through the pre-existing gap in an Iron Age cross-ridge dyke. Perhaps this was just for convenience, but it may well have been that the Roman engineers were following an ancient ridgeway route which had been in existence since the Bronze Age.

Near Eggardon Hillfort the road leaves the chalk high ground and drops onto the greensand, with its many small hills and valleys. Here its route must have been tortuous, and tracing it is very difficult. There is sufficient evidence to suggest that it passed through or near Bridport, Chideock, Morecombe Lake, Charmouth and Pen Cross, before leaving Dorset at Raymond's Hill (SY 329 963). Its route does not become entirely clear again till it reaches Axminster, where it parallels the Axminster bypass. A recent excavation at Hogchester Farm (SY 3355 9475) just north of Charmouth produced a short stretch of the road as it climbs Thistle Hill.

The second excavation on the Second Augustan Legion's trunk road took place in 1983 at SY 544 937 on South Eggardon Farm (briefly reported in *Dorset Proceedings* vol.105 for 1983, p.146). This revealed that the materials of the road were very different (*83*). Here it lies on the chalk, and the causeway was entirely of flint, quarried from the chalk nearby. The sloping sides were of chalk rubble (also from the quarries) but the running surface was of gravel clearly brought from some distance away, perhaps from Black Down near Portesham.

The dimensions of the road at Thorncombe Wood and Eggardon were remarkably similar, probably reflecting the work of the same team of soldiers.

82 The Roman road west from Dorchester passing through (left of picture) the pre-existing gate of an Iron Age enclosure

83 Excavation of the Roman road passing Eggardon hillfort

4 Dorchester–Ilchester

With the development of the Fosse Way frontier a connection was needed to the new fort at Ilchester, and this may have been built at the same time as the Exeter road. From Dorchester the road leaves by the west gate (there is no evidence of a north gate) and almost immediately leaves the Exeter road and heads north-west. After three miles it crosses the Frome Valley between Bradford Peverell and Stratton (the latter name indicating the presence of a 'street'). Its causeway across the flood plain was later incorporated into the water meadow system, with a water channel cut into the centre of the *agger*.

In these 3 miles there must have been five bridges over the aqueduct (see chapter 4). From here the road turned to a more northerly direction and now for the most part lies under the modern A37. It can however be seen following an independent route at Hyde House (near Frampton), at Holywell (near Evershot) and just to the east of Melbury Park. It leaves the county near Ryme Intrinseca (ST 572 100) on its way to Ilchester. Close to Ilchester the *agger* can still be seen clearly in the field immediately west of the modern road. Later this road in its civilian guise joined Dorchester and Ilchester, the two Romanised towns of the Durotriges.

5 Badbury–Bath

From Badbury Rings a road is known to have run northwards across country towards Bath. It is difficult to follow once it leaves Dorset and the chalk near Ashmore (ST 922 175), but it is heading for the Bath area and perhaps the early harbour at Sea Mills. It is tempting to visualise heavy equipment from Lake Farm moving towards the Bristol Channel by this route as the campaigning area moved farther north.

The famous aerial photograph shown in *Figure 80* shows the start of this road, and demonstrates that it is the last of the sequence of Dorset roads. The photograph shows the field immediately north of Badbury Rings, looking south. The sequence of the three roads involved is quite clear.

The earliest road (route 1) from Old Sarum to Lake Farm and Hamworthy runs up the left edge of the photograph and swings away to the left as it passes the Rings on its way south. This is clearer on the ground than on the photograph.

The second road (route 2) is the road diverting from route 1 towards Dorchester, and this can be seen from bottom left to top right just skimming the edge of the Rings. The Bath road (route 5) is third in the sequence, running from to mid-left to mid-bottom.

In understanding this it is important to realise that ploughing has removed almost all the road metal, leaving just the buried ditches. The Bath road's place in the sequence is clear, since its ditches do not cut through the existing Dorchester road which is still in use. The Dorchester road's ditches remain, buried originally in new metalling for the Bath road. The ditches can still be seen at the crossroads because the Bath road's metalling has been mostly ploughed away. This is an important point, which has often been misunderstood.

The late Norman Field (Field 1992) claimed that another road to Hod Hill also originated at this point. However, the present author attended the excavations involved in this claim and does not accept its existence.

12

THE END OF ROMAN RULE

The popular view of the end of Roman Britain used to be that a sudden decision was taken in Rome to withdraw, and that the legions which arrived in AD 43 packed their bags and marched to the ports, to the cheers of the assembled people. The reality was very much more complex.

For a start, Britain had been under Roman rule for nearly 400 years – the equivalent of the period from Tudor times to the present day. Britain was unquestionably part of the Roman world and shared in its relative prosperity. The departure of Roman armies was something to be feared, as it left the country exposed to attack from outside the frontiers. In Britain's case the threat came from the Picts of Scotland, the Scots of Ireland, and the Saxons and other groups from northern Europe.

The army itself had changed; no longer were the legions the dominant units. Some still existed (the Second Augustan Legion was at Richborough) but they were now small infantry regiments. Pride of place was held by cavalry regiments formed to face the attacks of horse-borne barbarians from central Europe.

Even the names of civil and military leaders had changed by the fourth century. The military commander on the frontier was known as the Duke of Britain (*Dux Britanniarum*) and the commander responsible for naval defences in the south-east was the Count of the Saxon Shore (*Comes Litoris Saxonici*). Britain was by now five smaller provinces grouped to form a single diocese and the civilian governor was called the vicar (*vicarius*).

A major crisis occurred in AD 367 when the Picts, the Scots and the Saxons apparently conspired (or so the Romans thought) to attack Britain at the same time, and the country was overrun. It could easily have been the end of Roman Britain. But somehow the central government, itself under severe pressure from barbarian attacks, managed to find the resources to rescue Britain. A senior general, Theodosius, spent two years restoring normality, and putting the coastal defences and Hadrian's Wall back in working order.

At this time in Dorset we have very little evidence of what was happening. There is however one sign of the dramatic changes caused by the end of Roman rule. Along the north-east boundary of Durotrigian territory ran Bokerley Dyke (*84*). It had a long and complex history in Iron Age times, but after the Roman conquest it became redundant.

84 Bokerley Dyke, the old Durotrigian frontier

The Roman trunk road to London (Ackling Dyke) passed through the old prehistoric frontier at Bokerley Junction, a little north of the hamlet of Woodyates. When it was constructed a suitable gap was made in the defences. At some time in the late fourth century or early in the fifth the road was blocked by an extension of the Iron Age dyke. Soon afterwards it was reopened and then closed again. We have a tantalising glimpse of the *civitas* of the Durotriges putting their old defences in order to protect themselves from the chaos in other parts of the province.

There is not enough evidence to say whether they were successful, though the absence of Saxons in Dorset till much later suggests they were. There would have been no soldiers in Dorset, but there may have been town militias to protect Dorchester and Ilchester, and others may have been armed for the occasion in spite of the Roman law which forbade it. Certainly neither towns nor villas show signs of violent destruction at this date.

Amazingly it is in this very period between the barbarian conspiracy and the end of Roman rule that the towns and villas in Dorset seem to have reached their greatest prosperity, and this is very difficult to explain, except by an influx of people trying to escape from more troubled areas.

At this time Britain was reasonably well defended. But between 383 and 407 troops were repeatedly withdrawn from Britain to help on the continent, or to intervene on behalf of British commanders who thought they could make a better job of the western emperorship than the man in command at the time. Magnus Maximus took the troops with him in 383, and left chaos behind him. Stilicho restored the situation in 396, only for the adventure to be repeated by Constantine III in 407.

At this point Roman control of Britain lapsed, and it becomes very difficult to know what happened in Britain in any detail. The traditional date for the end of Roman Britain is 410; in that year the *civitates* of Britain on their own account wrote to the emperor Honorius, explained their plight and what they were doing to help themselves. Honorius wrote back and told them to see to their own defence. Clearly by this time (probably in 407 or thereabouts) Roman officials had been withdrawn, the vicar's palace in London was empty, and the civil service left without a job.

At some point in the first decade of the fifth century coins of 402 were dropped in fireplaces built on the mosaics of Dewlish Villa; clearly the buildings were in use, but not in the grand style of its former owners. Nevertheless nothing violent happened. The villa had been cleared of all its possessions and the rooms were empty when weather and decay ultimately led to the collapse of the roof. Life in Dorchester and Ilchester must have gone on, the walls becoming especially significant. A Durotrigian army may even have manned the frontier at Bokerley Dyke.

But the whole complex economic structure was collapsing. No money meant a return to the prehistoric practice of barter. Food and shelter were the important things. The markets for pottery and stone products were inaccessible. The industries collapsed and their owners were no longer wealthy. The workers were out of a job, and did their best to look after their families. The materials for repairing buildings were not available, and the goods essential to the Roman way of life unobtainable. The feeling of being shut out of the familiar Roman world must have been depressing indeed.

As the years passed Dorset returned more and more to the pattern of life of its prehistoric past – which had never really disappeared in the countryside anyway. How long the towns survived we cannot yet tell. It must have been well into the fifth century and perhaps even longer. Neither Dorchester nor Ilchester have had major excavations in modern times in the town centre, which might give some clue as to events.

In the east Saxons and others had been settling for many years already, in some cases by arrangement, in others by force. But they did not reach the south-west in any numbers for another two centuries, and life in Dorset must have gone on. How long the *ordo* continued to meet in the *basilica* at Dorchester and struggled to keep control of events is impossible to say. Perhaps power came to rest in a single personable leader, though we know nothing of it in Dorset. We have tantalising glimpses of the struggle to keep the Saxons out. We hear of great leaders in Britain heading the resistance; Vortigern, Ambrosius Aurelianus and Arthur. Victories were won, including a famous one at Mount Badon, which may have been in Dorset.

At South Cadbury in Somerset, and at other sites in the south-west, evidence has recently been found of the old hillforts being reoccupied by these sub-Roman leaders (*85*). They can be dated, particularly by the wine jars they were importing from the Mediterranean. No such site has been found in Dorset yet, but no major hillfort excavations have taken place in recent years. Mediterranean pottery of the fifth or sixth centuries is said to have been found in Dorchester, but this is uncertain.

In the end Saxon armies and settlers overran Dorset, probably on a large scale in the early seventh century. After that a new story begins.

85 South Cadbury Castle. The white posts stand in the postholes of the fifth- or sixth-century hall

Archaeologists face great difficulties in studying the fifth and sixth centuries AD. After Roman rule ceased, official coins were no longer minted in the province or imported from the continent to pay the army or the civil service. The latest coins routinely found in excavations are of the House of Theodosius of the years 388-402. It is clear that after a few years there were not enough low-value coins in circulation for a monetary economy to continue.

In addition the mass production of pottery in Purbeck came to an end, presumably because the markets disappeared, including the lucrative army contracts. A few sherds are found in a coarser fabric than the earlier styles types, which may offer evidence for the closing years of the industry, but the evidence is far from certain.

Another problem is the location of archaeological sites of the period. Often this happens through field-walking, where a scatter of broken pottery gives an indication of an underlying site. If no pottery was available, people had to use containers of other materials such as wood, which in typical soil conditions will leave no trace. It must have made life difficult, and one can imagine ordinary pottery becoming quite valuable as users took great care not to break it. It may be that some of the Late Roman pottery we find in excavations was still in use long after it was made.

Over time, most of the Romano-British farms and hamlets also seem to have been abandoned, as people moved away to live at new sites. A recent excavation at Worth Matravers (Hinton 1998) showed how frustratingly difficult it is to chart the process of abandonment and shift. There, a Late Roman barn with a large grain-dryer built into it did not simply collapse; instead, the dryer was deliberately cobbled over to level it off

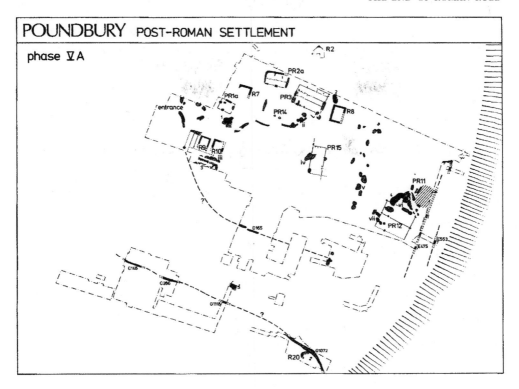

86 Plan of the post-Roman settlement at Poundbury, Dorchester. © *Dorset Natural History and Archaeological Society*

with the rest of the building – perhaps an indication that the farmers using the dryer were no longer under pressure to grow cereals intensively, but wanted a hard-standing for animals. The barn was probably already in a state of collapse when a single burial was inserted at one end. This grave was unmarked and soon forgotten, as a pit was dug that cut away the whole of the upper half of the body. The sequence of events is clear enough – but none of them can be dated, as the only objects in the features were fourth-century pottery sherds.

In Dorchester there is one important piece of almost dramatic evidence. At Poundbury (Green, C.S. 1987) on the site of the Roman extramural cemetery north-west of the town, slots and holes showed that at various times some 15 timber structures stood there, several on top of Roman burials (*86*). Some distinctive 'sunken-featured' buildings had involved digging a shallow, rectangular pit. There were grain-dryers, blacksmithing evidence and loom-weights used in weaving. There was certainly a substantial settlement there.

A few objects, such as combs, are similar in type to some found outside Dorset that are definitely post-Roman, and fifth- and sixth-century dates were obtained from radiocarbon dating. Poundbury is the only large excavation of a Dorset site that certainly dates from immediately after the Roman period. There is smaller-scale evidence from St

George's Road, Dorchester, where a 'sunken-featured' building could be contemporary with Poundbury's. That site was used in the fourth century, and probably like many others was not abandoned until well into the fifth or even later.

At a date which is impossible to define, the ruins of *Durnovaria* will have become impossible to live in, which is presumably why the small traces of post-Roman settlement are to be found in the suburbs such as Poundbury and Fordington.

There is a bigger site on the outskirts of Dorchester at Alington Avenue (Davies 2002), which seems to belong to the seventh/eighth century. There, too, there was Late Roman settlement, but then perhaps with an interlude before people moved back onto it. There must be many other rural sites to be found in Dorset; those around Dorchester have been traced because most twentieth-century development has happened there, leading to rescue excavations.

It was probably the early ninth century before Dorchester was re-founded as a Saxon town, still within its Roman walls. For a fuller discussion of the change to Saxon Dorset see David Hinton's book *Discover Dorset – Saxons and Vikings* (Hinton 1998).

PLACES TO VISIT

Ackling Dyke, Roman road Join it half a mile south-east of Handley roundabout on the A354 from Blandford to Salisbury (where the B3081 crosses – SU 016 164). The road can be followed from here south-west towards Badbury Rings for over 9 miles.

Badbury Rings. 4 miles north-east of Wimborne. Roman road junction beside Iron Age hillfort (ST 966034).

Bokerley Dyke, frontier earthwork The A354 crosses it at Bokerley Junction (SU 033 198), just beyond Woodyates on the way from Blandford to Salisbury.

Dorchester, aqueduct. Follows the Frome valley to the north-west of Dorchester to Frampton. It can best be seen west of Poundbury hillfort and in Fordington Bottom (SY 6791).

Dorchester, Carinus tombstone Original in St George's Church, Fordington (SY 699 905), replica in Dorset County Museum.

Dorchester, Dorset County Museum In High West Street; contains the major collection of archaeological material from the county including many Roman finds.

Dorchester, Maumbury Rings Where the Weymouth road crosses the railway (SY 690 899). Roman Amphitheatre.

Dorchester, town wall Surviving fragment (SY 689 906) just south of the Top o' Town roundabout.

Dorchester, town house Displayed behind County Hall (SY 689 909).

Hod Hill 4 miles north-west of Blandford on the A350 (ST 8510). Roman fort inserted into Iron Age hillfort.

Industry None of the industrial sites in Dorset are on display. Finds may be seen in the museums mentioned above.

Jordan Hill, Roman temple Near Bowleaze Cove, 2 miles east along the coast from Weymouth (SY 699 822). Foundations only to be seen.

Maiden Castle 2 miles south-west of Dorchester on the A354 (SY 6688). Scene of a possible assault by the Second Augustan Legion.

Maiden Castle, Roman temple The foundations of the temple (SY 672 885) are on view in the hillfort – see above.

Priest's House Museum, Wimborne Finds from the Tarrant Hinton Roman Villa, including the tombstone, the pump and the painted wall plaster.

South Cadbury Castle 10 miles north-east of Yeovil on the A303 (ST 6225). Iron Age hillfort reoccupied in the Late Roman period by King Arthur or someone like him.

Thorncombe Wood, Roman road 4 miles east of Dorchester near Higher Bockhampton. The road is visible for over a mile through Thorncombe Wood into Puddletown Forest, starting at SY 726 919.

Villas No Dorset villa is on view to the public. Finds can be seen and inquiries made about excavations in progress at the museums at Dorchester, Poole and Wimborne.

BIBLIOGRAPHY AND SOURCES
OF FURTHER INFORMATION

I SPECIFIC TO DORSET AND THE DUROTRIGIAN TRIBAL AREA

Alcock, L. 1972. *By South Cadbury is that Camelot.*

Coates, J.U. 1902. 'The water supply of Ancient Dorchester, dating probably from Roman times' *Dorset Proceedings*, vol. 22 for 1902, p.80.

Cosh, S.R. and Neal, D.S. 2004. *Roman Mosaics of Britain, Vol II The South-West.*

Cunliffe, B. 1987. *Hengistbury Head, Dorset*, vol. 1.

Davies, S.M. *et al.* 2002. *Excavations at Alington Avenue, Fordington, Dorchester, Dorset, 1984-87.*

Draper J. and Chaplin C. 1982. *Dorchester Excavations*, vol.1.

Drew, C.D. and Collingwood Selby, K.C. 1938. 'The Excavations at Colliton Park, Dorchester 1937-1938, first interim report' in *Dorset Proceedings*, vol. 59, p.1-14.

Drew C.D. and Collingwood Selby, K.C. 1939. 'The Excavations at Colliton Park, Dorchester, second interim report' in *Dorset Proceedings*, vol. 60, p.51-65.

Farwell, D.E. and Molleson, T.I. 1993. *Poundbury Vol.II: The Cemeteries.*

Field, N.H. 1992. *Dorset and the Second Legion.*

Foster, P. 1922. 'The Roman aqueduct at Dorchester' *Dorset Proceedings*, vol. 46 for 1922, p.1.

Graham, A. 2006. *Barton Field, Tarrant Hinton, Dorset: Excavations 1968-1984.* Dorset Natural History and Archaeological Society Monograph No 17.

Green, C.S. 1987. *Excavations at Poundbury Vol. I: The Settlements.*

Hinton, D. 1998. *Discover Dorset – Saxons and Vikings.*

Hutchins, J. 1863. *The History and Antiquities of the County of Dorset*, vol. II.

Leach, P. 2001. *Roman Somerset.*

Lucas, R.N. 1993. *The Romano-British Villa at Halstock, Dorset, Excavations 1967-1985.*

Lysons, S. 1817. *Reliquiae Britannico-Romanae*, vol. II.

Mick A. and Putnam, B. Forthcoming. *The Dewlish Roman Villa.*

Putnam, W.G. 1970. 'Dewlish Roman Villa, a trial excavation' *Dorset Proceedings*, vol. 91 for 1970, p.186-7.

Putnam, W.G. 1971. 'Second Interim report on excavations at Dewlish Roman Villa 1970' *Dorset Proceedings,* vol. 92 for 1971, p.146-7.

Putnam, W.G. 1972. 'Third Interim report on excavations at Dewlish Roman Villa 1971' *Dorset Proceedings*, vol. 93 for 1972, p.157-60.

Putnam, W.G. 1973. 'Fourth Interim report on excavations at Dewlish Roman Villa 1972' *Dorset Proceedings*, vol. 94 for 1973, p.81-6.

Putnam, W.G. 1974. 'Fifth Interim report on excavations at Dewlish Roman Villa 1973' *Dorset Proceedings*, vol. 95 for 1974, p.89-91.

Putnam, W.G. 1975. 'Sixth Interim report on excavations at Dewlish Roman Villa 1974' *Dorset Proceedings,* vol. 96 for 1975, p.59-62.

Putnam, W.G. 1976. 'Seventh Interim report on excavations at Dewlish Roman Villa 1975' *Dorset Proceedings*, vol. 97 for 1976, p.54-7.

Putnam, W.G. 1977. 'Dewlish' *Dorset Proceedings*, vol. 98 for 1977, p.54-5.

Putnam, W.G. 1978. 'Dewlish' *Dorset Proceedings*, vol. 99 for 1978, p.120.

Putnam, W.G. 1979. 'Dewlish' *Dorset Proceedings*, vol. 100 for 1979, p.113-14.

Putnam, W.G. 1992. 'Fieldwork and Excavation on the Dorchester Roman Aqueduct, Summer 1992' *Dorset Proceedings,* vol.114 for 1992, p.239-40.

Putnam, W.G. 1993. 'Fieldwork and Excavation on the Dorchester Roman Aqueduct, Summer 1993' in *Dorset Proceedings*, vol. 115 for 1993, p.152-3.

Putnam, W.G. 1994. 'Fieldwork and Excavation on the Dorchester Roman Aqueduct, Summer 1994' in *Dorset Proceedings*, vol. 116 for 1994, p.123-5.

Putnam, W.G. 1995. 'Fieldwork and Excavation on the Dorchester Roman Aqueduct, Summer 1995' in *Dorset Proceedings*, vol. 117 for 1995, p.128-31.

Putnam, W.G. 1996. 'Fieldwork and Excavation on the Dorchester Roman Aqueduct, Summer 1996' in *Dorset Proceedings*, vol. 118 for 1996, p.139-43.

Putnam, W.G. 1997. 'Dorchester Roman Aqueduct, Summer 1997' in *Dorset Proceedings*, vol. 119 for 1997, p.165-8.

Putnam, W.G. 1998. 'Dorchester Roman Aqueduct, Summer 1998' in *Dorset Proceedings*, vol. 120 for 1998, p.165-8.

Putnam, B. 1998. *Discover Dorset – The Prehistoric Age.*

Putnam, B. 2000. *Discover Dorset – The Romans.*

RCHM. 1970. *Historical Monuments in the County of Dorset* II, part 3.

Richmond, I.A.R. 1968. *Hod Hill.*

Sharples, N.M. 1991. *Maiden Castle, Excavations and Field Survey 1985-6.*

Sharples, N.M. 1991. *Maiden Castle.*

Smith, R.J.C. 1997. *Excavations along the Route of the Dorchester By-pass, Dorset, 1986-8.*

Tomlin R.S.O. and Hassall, M.W.C. 2000. 'Roman Britain in 1999, ii Inscriptions' *Britannia* vol. 31, p.433-4.

Wheeler, R.E.M. 1943. *Maiden Castle, Dorset.*

Woodward, P.J. 1993. *Excavations at Greyhound Yard, Dorchester 1981-4.*

Pamphlets

Putnam, B. 1999. *Roman Dorchester.* Dorset County Council.

Putnam, B. 2000. *The Roman Town House at Dorchester.* Dorset County Council.

For children

Putnam, M. 1997. *The Romans in Dorset Book 1: The Roman Conquest.*

Putnam, M. 1998. *The Romans in Dorset Book 2: Roman Dorchester.*

Information about Dorset itself appears mainly in the publications of the Dorset Natural History and Archaeological Society, who can be contacted at Dorset County Museum, High West Street, Dorchester DT1 1XA (01305 262735). Their journal *The Proceedings of the Dorset Natural History and Archaeological Society* has been published annually for well over 100 years. It contains a wealth of information about excavations and discoveries in Dorset. In addition the Society publishes a monograph series in which major excavation reports appear which are too bulky for the *Proceedings*. The Museum will be happy to send an up-to-date list of its publications on receipt of a stamped and addressed envelope.

The second main source for Dorset archaeology is the *Inventory of Historical Monuments in the County of Dorset* produced by the Royal Commission on Historical Monuments (England). This was published in five volumes by HMSO between 1952 and 1975. Although many years have passed since the publication of this great work, it remains an important starting point for any archaeological research in Dorset. Updated information can be obtained from the Historic Environment Record (formerly the Sites and Monuments Record) which can be consulted at the Dorset History Centre (formerly the Dorset Record Office) 01305 250550.

As a starting point for aerial survey, consult *Dorset, A Photographic Atlas* a CD published by Dorset County Council in 2000 (www.dorset-cc.gov.uk).

For internet research, a good starting point is the website of the Dorset Natural History and Archaeological Society, www.dor-mus.demon.co.uk.

2 GENERAL BACKGROUND FOR IRON AGE AND ROMAN BRITAIN

Bédoyère, de la, G. 1991. *The Buildings of Roman Britain.*

Branigan, K. and Miles, D. 1988. *The Economies of Romano-British Villas.*

Cunliffe, B. 1974. *Iron Age Communities in Britain.*

Cunliffe, B. 1983. *Danebury, Anatomy of an Iron Age Hill fort.*

Dark, K. and P. 1997. *The Landscape of Roman Britain.*

Darvill, T. 1987. *Prehistoric Britain.*

Davies, H. 2002. *Roads in Roman Britain.*

Frere, S.S. 1987. *Britannia* (third edition).

Frere. S.S. and St Joseph, J.K.S. 1983. *Roman Britain from the Air.*

Henig, M. 1984. *Religion in Roman Britain.*

Margary, I.D. 1967. *Roman Roads in Britain* (third edition).

Peddie, J. 1987. *Invasion, the Roman Conquest of Britain.*

Percival, J. *The Roman Villa.*

Reynolds, P.J. 1987. *Ancient Farming.*

Rivet, A.L.F. 1969. *The Roman Villa in Britain.*

Salway, P. 1993. *The Oxford Illustrated History of Roman Britain.*

Scott, E. 1993. *A Gazetteer of Roman Villas in Britain.*

Thomas, C. 1986. *Celtic Britain.*

Wacher, J. 1995. *The Towns of Roman Britain* (second edition).

Webster, G. 1985. *The Roman Imperial Army* (third edition).

Map

Ordnance Survey. 2001. *Historical Map and guide – Roman Britain* (fifth edition 2001).

Journal

The journal that deals with Roman Britain in general is *Britannia*, published annually by the Society for Promotion of Roman Studies at Senate House, Malet Street, London WC1E 7HU. Members can also consult the journal online at www.romansociety.org

INDEX